Richard is a husband, father and funeral director. His time is devoted either to his work, at which he clocks way more hours than he should, or to his children and the occasional book in the back garden.

Born in the UK, Richard moved to Sydney twenty years ago after marrying his Australian wife. He has been a funeral director for ten years, appearing in the 2018 SBS documentary *The Secret Life of Death*. He has also been interviewed on ABC Radio multiple times about his job and the profound satisfaction it brings him.

AFTER THE WORST HAS HAPPENED

RICHARD GOSLING

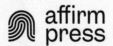

affirm
press

First published by Affirm Press in 2024
Bunurong/Boon Wurrung Country
28 Thistlethwaite Street
South Melbourne VIC 3205
affirmpress.com.au
10 9 8 7 6 5 4 3 2 1

This work was made on the unceded land of the Bunurong/Boon Wurrung peoples
of the Kulin Nation. Affirm Press pays respect to their Elders past and present.

 A catalogue record for this
book is available from the
National Library of Australia

ISBN: 9781923022379 (paperback)
Cover design by Alex Ross © Affirm Press
Typeset in Garamond Premier Pro by J&M Typesetting
Proudly printed and bound in Australia by the Opus Group

Dedicated to Melinda, Sandy and Tilda

And to those who turned the corner:
Chris Murray, Odette Maddern, Steve Gray, James Iles
and 'Great' Uncle Steve

Contents

Monday Morning

Death is waiting. From our first breath, death sits patiently somewhere along our road. Death anticipates our arrival but doesn't hurry us along. We'll get there in due time; every tick and every tock brings us closer. No matter how we phrase it, how we dress it up, celebrate it or try to deny it, death is the closing of all our stories.

When our moment comes, we will turn the corner and death will stand to greet us.

~

I'm first in at the funeral home, as I usually am, a shade after 7am.

The radio has played me in to work, I've parked the car and I've disabled the alarms. I've unlocked the front door and spun the sign around to say 'Open'. It's rare, but not unheard of, that someone walks through the door this early. There may be ashes to collect or a death certificate to pick up. Or they could be what we call a 'walk in' – someone passing who needs to talk about an upcoming death, or one

1

that has already happened, someone with questions they need to ask and who needs reassurance.

Monday morning is always dictated by whatever the weekend has brought to us. We try not to have services on a Monday as, for one thing, it is the priests' day off, and for another we never know what the weekend will have been like. On Sunday night, whoever is on call sends around a text message: *three for the chevra kadisha* (the Jewish mortuary, which we look after during Shabbat), *two for us*. It's like a soccer score at a weekend game.

Last night it was three for us, none for them.

Three new cases to be divided between us. Three deceased as yet unknown to me, their names on the 'first call sheets' that we travel with. (These are A4 forms contaning a series of headings for essential information relating to each new case, written at whatever time of day or night they are called in to us.) Three people who died between Friday at 4.30pm and this Monday morning. Died while those of us not on call were doing laundry, shopping, taking the kids to the cinema, taking our partners to dinner, leading normal weekends. Meanwhile, one colleague spent the weekend on call, close to the phone. A clipboard and pen ready to take down the details of the people who had been moving towards their time since birth. People who'd gone through their lives not thinking about death nearly as much as I do – hopefully.

When the first call comes, we hear families struggling to adjust to a now past tense. Saying he *did* instead of he *does*. Saying she *would* instead of she *will*. They *had* instead of they *have*. Then struggling more when we ask for the deceased's name. It's hard to name the dead when they were so recently alive.

Medical causes of death have to be obtained, all with their facts detailed coolly. Heart problems. Cancer. Dementia. Strokes.

Accidents. Impacts. Crashes. One of these will perhaps match the cause on the form that will be filled out for me some day yet to come. Written in scrawled biro by a doctor.

Birth certificate to death certificate, and then everything we do sandwiched in between them. Every document we develop, tax return we complete, driver's licence, speeding ticket, parking fine, bank statement, contract, so many pieces of paper with the name we were given on our birth certificate spread out in our wake. So much done in the chaos, ennui, exhilaration and exhaustion of our lives.

I make coffee, watch the bubbles form like eyes winking at me. I switch off the overnight mode on the phones, and I feel the funeral home cool around me as the air conditioning chases the heat of the weekend away.

The large TV screen with the three security-camera feeds flickers on. Reception: empty, the door closed. The parking bays out the back: my black car huddled in the middle space. The chapel downstairs: the rows of chairs and the open curtains – and I am convinced again that I see a woman sitting in the front row, her head down, knees together, dressed in black, quietly waiting for a funeral to begin. She's not there, though. She never is.

Right now, there are three people whose mother, best friend, cousin or neighbour has died. People who are waiting for us to call. People possibly still raw with the loss, jet-lagged by it, not sure what to do with themselves.

They are waiting for us to call, now that the worst has happened for someone they care about, now that the first Monday has come without them. Now that death is no longer waiting.

Wet Socks

'Everything we do we do slowly; we move slowly, we speak slowly, we never rush. Anyone watching us sees calm, certainty and control. Most importantly, we react slowly. Never run or look flustered.'

The first conductor I ever worked with in funerals told me this. The conductor is the person in charge of the service itself. They will usually have four other people with them. The second in command is the hearse driver, and then there are the two bearers. At a service in a funeral home chapel there are usually only two staff in attendance – a conductor and one bearer. The bearer's role is to take signatures for the memorial book, hand out the orders of service and direct people to the bathrooms, while the conductor liaises with the family. The bearer then moves to the AV desk and plays any music or video tributes while the conductor watches the attendees, who sometimes cough, sob or even faint. The conductor is on hand with water, tissues and first-aid training.

At one of my first funerals, people were coming up the steps and my instinct was to rush to help every unsteady person. The conductor put his hand on my arm and gave me the instruction. Move slowly, act slowly. If we appear calm, those attending will be reassured.

In other words, glide smoothly through the water, and never let them see you paddling.

~

My wet-sock Wednesday came a few months later. I was forty years old, and had been working in the business for less than a year.

I was standing outside a crematorium chapel with a large overspill crowd from the service inside. The doors were wide open, and the eulogy could just about be heard over the general clamour of a large group of people. This was before outdoor screens broadcast everything that goes on inside. The family hadn't wanted a church and were adamant that the crematorium would be fine, despite it only seating around a hundred. People were shushing each other but still whispering, still checking phones or stepping further back on the grass to have a smoke. Flicking their ash on the small plots where human cremated remains were buried.

If the crowd inside laughed, then the group outside would try to guess what the comment had been and laugh along. A ripple would occur, confusion, suggestions, then laughter.

They were gathered around the hearse, and I was trying to keep them marshalled so they didn't spread too far or make so much noise that we'd disturb the smaller service in the chapel to the left.

The service moved towards a sense of an ending, and I saw the side doors open. One of my colleagues, today's conductor, nodded to me from within the chapel, and I nodded back. Always keep in the eye-line of the conductor, I'd been taught. You can't shout instructions across a church or chapel, so you are constantly looking for eye contact with your team, nods to the left or right, subtle gestures of instruction.

The family appeared slowly, crying softly, and the music from inside flowed over us. Frank Sinatra assured us that, yet again, he had done it his way. The crowd relaxed now that they weren't missing anything, knowing they were getting closer to the wake and the beer, the ashtrays and anecdotes. A flutter of applause started and stopped as the chapel slowly disgorged, giving us a crowd of roughly 150 now, which we would need to gently disperse. I could see the next hearse waiting just around the bend.

The unfortunate thing about crematorium services is that there is often another funeral right on your heels. Another funeral home waiting to carry their coffin in, to set up their table and memorial book and orders of service outside. If one service overruns, then the next service and the next after that, and so on through the day, are all impacted. We always try to run to time, and we try to disperse our crowds.

Being left with the cathartically released mourners from the first funeral while the next group are arriving can be awkward. Their tears have fallen, their songs have been sung and their grief has been felt. After the service they are ready for a chat about what a good fella the deceased was, how they really *did* do it their way, while the mourners arriving for the next service are trying to find their feet, their space and their time. We stay until our attendees have dispersed as an act of good grace to the next funeral home coming in. We call out, 'Ladies and gentlemen, thank you for your attendance today, but please be aware there is another funeral commencing shortly. Please move along out of respect for the next family coming in.' Sometimes it works first time, other times we stand with our arms up to usher folk, calling out, asking them to move on, but they stay, and they talk, and they don't see. Sometimes they become annoyed at the conveyer belt feeling of one in, one out, but we don't leave until they have moved along and we know that the next family have their space and their time.

On this Wednesday, I had just started calling out, lifting my arms and gesturing to usher the crowd towards the condolence rooms across the gardens, when behind me I heard a scream, and then a heavy thud. I spun and saw a man on the floor twitching violently. His arms were clenched to his chest, his knees together bent upward. His head was snapping back and forth, and people were leaping back, forming a circle around him, before they looked to me. The black suit and the name badge. People look for a uniform to deal with the unexpected.

I stepped forward and knelt beside the man as his spasms continued. Close to his head was a metal litter bin and I slipped off my suit jacket and balled it up, wedging it between the man's head and the corner of the bin.

'Does he need CPR?' a woman close by asked.

'No, he's breathing. I think he's having a fit,' I replied.

The letters C, P and R caught alight and burnt through the crowd. One of my colleagues could see what was happening, and I saw them talking to the concierge and pointing to us. The concierge nodded, and I guessed an ambulance would be on the way. Meanwhile, a large man was pushing through the crowd in a pseudo-suit – black jeans, black boots, black T-shirt and a black tracksuit top. He was stretching out his arms and shouting, 'I know CPR, I know CPR.'

The man on the floor was still now. His fit had come to its end, and he was softly chewing at the air, his eyes closed, blood trickling from a bite on his tongue.

'It's okay,' I called. 'We don't need CPR.'

The man seemed not to hear me. He strode on through the crowd, repeating that he knew what to do, he knew CPR.

'He knows CPR,' the woman close by told me.

'I understand, but this man doesn't need CPR.'

She smiled at me. 'Maybe CPR would help?'

The man was moving towards us now, and I held up a hand and tried to catch his eye. 'It's okay, my friend, he's breathing and has a pulse, we don't need CPR.'

Ignoring me, the man knelt and tried to roll the man at my feet onto his back.

'It's okay,' I said again. 'He's breathing and he has a pulse. He's had a fit. There's an ambulance on the way.'

The black-clad man looked up at me and smiled. 'I know CPR,' he said confidently.

He moved to place his hands on the man's chest.

I dropped to my knees again and put my hands in the way. 'Sir, he's breathing, he has a pulse. He doesn't need CPR. CPR will cause him harm. He's okay.'

The man went to perform a chest compression and looked confused and angry as I took his wrists and pulled them gently but firmly back. *Just act slowly, just be calm.* I don't think I am so calm anywhere else in life, but I was learning to be so around the bereaved.

'He's breathing. If you start chest compressions, you're going to do far more harm than good.'

The crowd watched. Waited.

'How'd you know? You a doctor?'

I rolled the man onto his side into the recovery position.

'I'm not a doctor. I'm a funeral director,' I said.

The man dropped his hands, stood and brushed off his knees and nodded. 'Well, that's okay, then.' He turned away and then stopped, looking at the gathered crowd. 'It's okay,' he shouted. 'The man's breathing, he's going to be okay.'

Applause started, and the man in the black pseudo suit held his arms up like a champion and then gave a few short bows.

The man on the ground was blinking now, his eyes unfocused, mouth still gnawing slowly at the air.

Someone from the crowd suddenly gave a nervous laugh, and I looked down to see a warm wave of urine washing around my boots.

I remembered my housemate Jim back in London. He has epilepsy and he'd told me several times never to try to jam anything in his mouth if he was fitting – he'd likely bite my fingers off if I tried. 'Just make sure I don't slam into anything if you can. Oh, and have some towels ready.'

'Towels?' I'd asked Jim.

'Yeah,' he said, sighing. 'Sometimes I piss myself after a fit.'

Pseudo-suit looked back at me and smiled. 'Ambo's coming,' he said, and I saw the blue flashing lights coming around from the left.

Move slowly, act slowly. I lifted my feet from the puddle and reached for my jacket, then stepped – slowly – backwards, feeling my socks now warm and wet.

'Ladies and gentlemen,' I said, making my voice calm and steady, 'if we could please move along now and make room for the ambulance. Thank you.'

First Interview

When I was twenty-one, in the mid-1990s, I saw an advert in the local paper for a crematorium operator. At this point in life I'd made it eight miles from my home town in England (Sandy, where my son gets his name from) to the next market town, Bedford. This was before online recruitment sites like Seek, in the days when jobs were advertised once a week in newspaper notices, to be drawn around in black biro. The job came with a house in a graveyard and an annual suit allowance. To my mind the job would mean living a life akin to the movie *Return of the Living Dead*: living in a graveyard with rolling mists over tombstones, distant wolf-howls, bats flapping across full moons, flickering hallways, and 1980s music and hair.

Professional, empathetic, patient and *mature*, the job notice said. Being twenty-one, I wasn't yet any of those things. But a job in a graveyard – that would go down well with the girls in nightclubs. Being twenty-one, my interests were heavily focused on girls and Stephen King novels, and, truth be told, the novels came first on that list. There could be no harm in applying, I reasoned.

At the time, I was already dwindling away as an admin assistant in the public service, feeling my identity being eroded one day at a time, alongside talk of how, maybe in three years, I could apply to be an admin officer, and then a few years after that I could look to becoming an executive officer, and then, if I worked steadily and well, I could end my career as a senior executive officer. AA to AO to EO to SEO.

This was the dream of a career civil servant. A career of hallways and of gossip and of nothing ever changing. Something about this crematorium job read to me (once I let my unrealistic ideas of horror movies and novels slip away) as peaceful and unique and far from this alphabet chase that I was currently on.

Every other job on the 'Situations Vacant' page sounded like monotonous, office-based, paper-churning repetition, couched in buzzwords like key performance indicators and benchmarking. Sterile halls and ant-farm desks – the kinds of jobs I ended up in for the next decade and a half anyway, and am now hugely thankful to have far in my rear-view mirror.

I sent in an application as professionally, empathetically, patiently and maturely as I could. I then tried to forget all about it. My life outside work at the time was mainly spent reading said Stephen King novels in a sharehouse with three other guys. We had empty cigarette boxes blu-tacked to the wall like small shelves, with Kinder egg toys displayed on them – our version of *The Young Ones*.

When, three weeks later, I received a sombre phone call asking me to come in for an interview, I was ecstatic. I decided there and then that I would nail the interview and move into the graveyard residence within a week.

Being twenty-one, brash and British, and having no sense of forward planning whatsoever, the only suit I owned was a mail-order catalogue light (bright) green affair made of something highly combustible, which I had worn all of twice since buying. In fact, when it first arrived I'd realised that it didn't fit but had forgotten to return it, it being just too much work to deal with the admin. It was too tight in the shoulders and too loose at the waist. Never buy a suit from a mail-order catalogue; it's the definition of a pig in a poke.

I only had one white shirt, also a questionable fit, and the only tie I possessed had Roger Rabbit on it. With the jacket done up, I was confident the tie would simply seem dark blue. I accepted the interview and saw my future shining brightly in the shadows of death and gravestones, perfumed by cider and cigarettes.

I tucked in my shirt, cinched my belt, tied Roger Rabbit around my neck in a bad schoolboy knot and buttoned my jacket. One of my shoelaces snapped, and I had to unlace it to a lower set of rings in order to tie it. No one would notice, though. Light (bright) green combustible suit, Roger Rabbit hopefully hidden, jacket too tight and trousers too loose, I was ready for the future.

My girlfriend drove me to the interview, and around then my nerves started creeping in. I don't think many of us really learn to talk until we are in our forties. Small talk is an art. Confidence is very hard to come by, and only arrives after experience – lots of experience. At that time, I had absolutely no experience beyond a dingy lounge with three guys and a bag of takeaway kebabs.

I'd worked in a few factories, once gluing cardboard dump bins together for supermarkets. I'd accidentally sprayed molten glue over one hand on the first day, and the guy next to me had said, 'Ah well, let it dry, and then peel it off.' I'd watched in pain for a few seconds as the skin underneath puckered and split while the glue set. He'd shown me his own hands, flecked with white mounds and scars from molten glue.

I'd worked scanning old insurance files for fading British celebrities, spending my days reading about how this comedian mustn't have a minibar in any room he stayed in, and how that singer was to be closely monitored for substance abuse. None of these jobs had gone well, and, at this time in my life, I was lost in the reprographics room of a government office, spending my days reading novels about dragons and vampires when not pressing the big green button for large print jobs.

'Have you thought about the interview questions?' my girlfriend asked me as she parked on the gravel outside the cemetery office.

'Um'.

'Do you know what you are going to say?'

'Er'.

She smiled, kissed me and said she was sure I'd do well. 'Maybe try not to say um and er. You look very – well – kind of – nice,' she said. She glanced at the red-brick building and the chimneys and told me she'd come back in forty minutes; she didn't want to hang around a cemetery. Then she sprayed me on the back of the head with a scent she said suited me, and I climbed out of the car.

For the first time, I wondered why I wanted to be here, in a cemetery, given my girlfriend's quite natural reaction to it. Looking around at the gravestones and the trimmed lawns, at the old trees swaying softly and the wrought-iron gate down the gravel driveway, I wondered why this felt so comfortable. It wasn't the Stephen King novels or the Edgar Allan Poe aspirations; there was something about the cemetery and the crematorium that felt correct. Felt like somewhere that I should be working.

A lady with tightly permed grey hair opened the door and made a very quick up and down assessment of me. I hoped she hadn't seen Roger Rabbit. I introduced myself, and she nodded and ushered me in. In retrospect, I know I failed the interview in that instant. Her opinion would carry great weight with the two men I was to meet. Retrospect is a cruel thing, but it's rarely wrong.

'There's an interview going on ahead of yours. While that is finishing, I'll show you the house.'

She led me down the hallway past a closed dark door, beyond which I could hear a muted and hopefully awful interview taking place. She opened a door and explained: 'The home is part of the main building. Everything beyond this door is part of the residence.'

A narrow hall led to a flight of stairs, and I followed her up, feeling my half-tied shoe slipping on my foot. She showed me a furnished lounge, a master bedroom and a smaller second bedroom. There was kitchen that I could destroy food in and, from every window, there were graves.

She explained that visitors to the cemetery over the weekends would often knock at the residence and ask for help finding a loved one. She explained that the resident of the house would open and lock the gates each day and deal with any and all weekend enquiries. There was a large map on the wall by the door of the cemetery, a chaotic grid of graves that I was keen to learn. As she talked, I nodded and said very little, thinking of the unbeatable opening line I would have for any conversation: 'Hey, yeah, I live in a cemetery.'

'So?' she asked me.

'I'm sorry?'

'So, the residence, does it seem acceptable to you?'

I nodded. 'Yes. I mean, my current place is a real shi— ... is a shared house.'

She looked at me for a long time before continuing. 'You'd be living here alone. Only family members can stay with you.'

I flashed on Jack Torrence in *The Shining*. 'That's okay. I'm fine on my own. It would give me time to write.'

She tilted her head. 'You're a writer?'

'Well, I hope to be. One day.'

She looked extremely unconvinced, but then we heard a cough from downstairs and a man's voice call out, 'We're ready down here.'

She smiled at me thinly. 'Well, they're ready for you,' she said. And then added, in a tone I look back on as sarcastic, 'Good luck.'

The interview is a blur. A dreadful blur.

I know they asked me if I had experienced death in my family and I mumbled something incomprehensible about my grandmother dying of a stroke when I was four and me wearing a cowboy suit when I went to see her in hospital in the hours before she passed.

They asked me if I was good with working in a team, and I went on an unimaginable tangent about a dispute I'd recently had with a co-worker who had said he wanted to kill me for a bad joke I'd made about how the trousers he was wearing looked like MC Hammer pants. I think I was hoping to show I could manage relationships. All I showed was that I was likely the only person in history to use the phrase 'Hammer time!' in a job interview, especially at a crematorium. Somewhere along the way, the two people interviewing me stopped taking notes and set their pens aside.

'Richard, tell me, please, why do you want this job?' one of them asked me. I went to reach for my glass of water and my jacket popped open, allowing Roger Rabbit to swing out and wave.

'I, uhm, I ... I think I could make a real difference here.'

An eyebrow raised. 'A difference? How, exactly? Are you going to bring our residents back to life?'

They both chuckled.

'Well,' I said, honestly thinking I was in on the joke, 'my grandfather is a faith-healer. And – oh – he thinks he is Jesus.' This last part I said in a rush.

This was true, Grandad *was* a faith-healer, and he *did* think he was Jesus, or the new Jesus due our way soon. They greeted this with silence broken only by the click of their pens as they retracted the nibs.

I scrambled my way back up, stumbling over my tongue as I added, 'But I don't see him much, and, uhm, I don't, uhm, obviously, think I am Jesus. I don't even believe in Jesus. Though, I mean, obviously I do believe ... in my grandfather, I mean. But not in God. I don't think. I mean, I'm not sure. I'm sorry, could you please ... what was the question?'

The interview ended.

They'd written hardly anything on their pads about me. One of them walked me to the door. Vaguely hopeful, I said, 'I could start within two weeks.' He smiled and thanked me and said they'd let me know as soon as they could. They didn't contact me at all, but a week later they readvertised the job and at the bottom in bold capitals they had printed, **PREVIOUS APPLICANTS NEED NOT REAPPLY.**

At least the guy ahead of me didn't get the job either.

~

From there I spent six or seven years moving up from reprographics (AA) to work with civil engineers in support roles (AO). On an IT training course one day, I realised I was still cripplingly shy when it came to the inevitable 'Introduce yourself and tell us something you did this last weekend' moment that preceded the training course.

My throat went dry, and every word I'd ever learnt left my brain.

I sought the trainer out at break time and asked him how I could do what he did for a living. I had to reintroduce myself as he had no memory of me being on the course, given I had failed to reply to the icebreaker question with anything memorable – or comprehensible. He gave me an email address where I could send my résumé and asked me why I wanted the job.

'Because it looks like it would terrify me,' I said.

When I eventually got the interview, he was there. He smiled and asked if I was terrified. I was in the middle of London, a long way from the fields that I had grown up around.

I nodded and said, 'Absolutely. Absolutely terrified. But it's kind of fun, isn't it?'

IT training didn't take the shyness out of me, but it taught me to mask it, to hide it behind a persona, a better-knotted tie and a suit bought from a shop, not a catalogue. I did have a lot of fun as well. I taught classes across the UK and parts of Europe, and my cemetery interview became a distant and amusing anecdote.

When I decided to move lock and stock to London, my father gave me one piece of advice: be wary of Australian girls. After a few years there, I ignored his advice and fell in love with Melinda – an Australian girl.

Mel and I married, and eventually relocated to Sydney – by way of a six-month honeymoon stint working in Cambodia. Once again, I was terrified, but also having fun.

One day in Phnom Penh without Mel, who was teaching in the village where we were living, I was asked if I wanted to smoke. I said no. Did I want to shoot? (The man mimed injecting his arm.) I said no. Did I want a young woman? No. A young man? No. Did I want a fight? (He shadow-boxed.) I said no. Then he asked me, 'Do you want to blow up a cow?' I didn't, but I was fascinated that I could if I wanted to.

When I said no again, he slapped his forehead and asked me, 'Well, what do you want?'

To which I could only answer, 'To buy some dumplings and get home to my wife.'

He marched away laughing at me, and I ducked into Western Union and withdrew money, then went and bought Mel's dumplings, and then got on the two-hour coach back to our village. Halfway there, the coach stopped and let on a vendor, and suddenly everyone on the bus had a plastic bag full of palm-sized spiders, deep-fried in oil. The Khmers on the bus offered them to me enthusiastically. I shrank back in my seat and tried to get my head around quite how far from home I was. Then I remembered I had left home, and wasn't really sure where any sense of permanence was any more. A small child thrust a fried spider at me and laughed when I shuddered. He then bit into its body and chewed joyfully.

I was a long way from home.

I was further away still once we landed in Australia. I was starting over and struggling to find a job. I had no university degree, which was something that hadn't seemed to matter in the UK, but which was apparently essential in Sydney. I was also struggling to find friends. All my old ones were left behind in London and I was suddenly thirty, swamped in sunshine, living by a beach (though unable to swim) and getting sunburnt each time I went outside.

After a while, I found my way into technical administrative work (same old AA, AO, EO nonsense as before) and slowly began making friends, and my struggles became smaller. In my first years in Sydney, I got lost repeatedly; had my boxer shorts stolen off of the washing line one day (by a man I hope I never bump into); fell into a wombat hole; lost my wallet in another wombat hole and reached in to retrieve it (without knowing how dangerous that was); fell into a hand-dug campsite toilet; and had to be hypnotised to stop myself screaming at spiders.

Then half-planned and unplanned and *oh well here we go*, we were on the way to becoming parents.

Prior to a pre-natal class one day, I impressed my wife by changing a flat car tyre.

'I honestly didn't think you'd be able to do that!' Mel told me.

Having a wife with low expectations makes for a happy marriage.

Everything was still unsettling, but I'd learnt to say *mate*, and people seemed to treat me a little nicer for it.

Then time folded. Childbirth and child raising and sleepless nights and gastro, and then the crazy idea that now we had one child, we really should have another.

We had the easiest, sweetest little boy, so why not have a second child? What could possibly go wrong?

Toes

Mel shook me awake in the middle of the night. Being woken up when you shouldn't be never feels right, though years later as a funeral director I would become very used to it. That night in 2009, though, with the urgency she was shaking me with, I felt instantly on guard. The last time she had woken me this way had been when she'd found a window open that shouldn't have been when she got up to feed our son during the night. We'd gradually worked out, in a reluctant suburban way, that the only way that window could be open was if someone had opened it, and neither of us had – so we'd been broken in to. This led to swinging out of bed and slowly exploring the place, but doing it loudly, and then having the awful sinking moment of seeing our back door wide open to the night and the night being darker than I had ever known it to be before.

'What is it?' I sat up in bed.

'It's Tilda,' she said, and then told me she had been playing a 'Hospital' game with the kids earlier in the day. She'd listened to our son's heart, and it sounded perfectly normal. Then she'd placed her head on our never-smiling, always-scowling, angry daughter's chest and, 'It just sounded wrong.' This was the rush of whispered information coming from the other side of the bed in darkness.

Mel asked if we could go and listen to it now.

'Nothing ever makes sense at night,' I said. 'And if it sounds wrong, there's nothing we can do right now. She's warm, she's well, she's alive. Maybe we just let her sleep, and we'll check in the morning?'

There was a heavy silence.

'I guess,' Mel said, but she didn't go back to sleep. Neither did I. We both lay silently, wide awake, the bed no longer comfortable, and the night outside growing louder. Usually, the sound of the ocean would lull us to sleep. On this night, it sounded like brittle things being crushed underfoot. Finally, we swung out of bed around 2am and walked through to the kids' room.

I lifted Tilda up as she slept, face creased into her standard state of barely supressed anger, and placed my ear to her eighteen-month-old chest. I wanted it to be nonsense; I wanted to hand her to Mel and say there was nothing wrong. Tilda's heart, though, didn't sound right at all. Instead of the healthy beat in my son's chest, Tilda's heartbeat had a wet, sucking sound. A drawing liquid noise, as though fluid were being pulled into a water pistol and then pushed out again while submerged.

'Well?'

Mel was standing behind me. Our son, Sandy, was deeply asleep in his bed. Tilda was beginning to grouch in my arms, but grouch beautifully. Warmly. Clearly safe and alive.

'It doesn't sound like it should.'

I felt things start to liquify. My daughter was here, though, pink and awake and now scowling at me. Tilda's first word had been 'No'. Mel insists that it was 'Mum', but I remember it as 'No'. Tilda followed that up with 'Go away'. After that came 'Mum' and 'Dad'. Her first sentences were, 'No, go away, Mum,' and then, 'No, go away, Dad.' She was a furious Sid Vicious of a baby. Completely alive and completely pissed off. As wrong as her heart sounded, she was in my arms and wriggling and, given she was now awake, wanting to be fed.

She seemed completely fine, but her chest sounded wrong.

It couldn't be that bad, though, could it?

~

'We're going to see a specialist at three, can you be there?'

During the day Mel had seen our GP, who had immediately agreed that things didn't sound right. The doctor had been reassuring; she'd said it was likely a hole in the heart and that it would close itself as Tilda grew, as these things often did. It wasn't uncommon, she said. To be on the safe side, though, things would move up the ladder a little. We had a rush appointment arranged with a paediatrician at Prince of Wales Hospital in Randwick, and I left work early and caught the bus there.

The paediatrician, who looked like Santa Claus and gave off a sense of complete reassurance, ushered us in and congratulated Mel on being the first mother in his experience ever to hear a VSD – ventricular septal defect – in a baby. This kind of thing was normally picked up at checks after birth, but not to worry, things would be okay, it would likely close as Tilda grew. He said all the same things the other doctor had. He was in awe of Mel's ear, but was certain that 'It sounds far worse than it likely is.' I think he called her some kind of super-mum.

Mel and the kids were due to go away the next day. Were they okay to fly to Byron Bay?

Of course, said the doctor. There was no need to worry. He winked at me and told me to enjoy a bit of alone time. He congratulated Mel again on hearing the hole, and we left – worried, but nowhere near as much as we had been.

~

Mel and the kids flew away. I was to have a few days to try to write a book. This was something I had been trying to do most of my life, starting when I was eight years old and attempted to rewrite *Star Wars* on a spiral notepad, cunningly changing Luke's name to Henry and giving the characters laser boomerangs rather than lightsabres – something I think I'd also lifted, from the fantasy movie *Krull*.

I had an idea for a story, and Byron was better off without me eating its lentils and yeast flakes. I would stay home, write like Hemingway, drink like Hemingway, and then eat like Hemingway and watch 1980s action movies in a Hemingway-esque manner – maybe even sneak in a Hemingway cigarette as the night sky brooded above.

After a day or so, I abandoned the writing. It simply wasn't working. Sentences drooped like cold spaghetti. Plots dissolved into stupidity. Exhausted with facing the blank page, I took myself to the cinema to see the movie *Watchmen*. There was just me and one other guy in the theatre. He was large and had two tubs of popcorn and a drink the size of a semi-trailer. He looked like Comic Book Guy from *The Simpsons*. This is what my life had become: sitting in a huge movie theatre watching a comic book movie soundtracked by a comic book guy constantly chewing. Then my phone buzzed.

'I'm in the cinema,' I said in a whisper, and my wife rushed to speak over me.

'I'm in an ambulance, I need to talk to you now.'

I rushed outside saying, 'Okay, hold on a moment, hold on.' Then, standing in the hallways of the cinema, I listened.

Tilda had fallen into the embers of the fire they'd had the night before. She was badly burnt on both hands. They were rushing to Brisbane Hospital from the smaller health centre in Mullumbimby. It was bad. Mel's voice was broken and hurried.

'Should I drive to you?' The cinema hallway stretched out in front of me, and the carpet seemed to tug me downwards. I felt myself shrinking, felt the quiet of the cinema press on me.

No, it was better if I stayed down here. Sandy would fly home in a day or so. Mel didn't know when she and Tilda would be back.

My son, fly home. Jesus, he was only three.

'Is it bad?'

'Yes. Yes, it is. Look, I've got to go, I'll call you when we get to Brisbane. I've got to—'

The call ended. I stood there, not knowing what to do. I turned in slow circles, my adult circuits not connecting. I was wanting to be told what to do. Drive to Brisbane. Go home. Give blood. Someone just had to tell me what to do.

Looking back, it is insane that I went back into the movie, but I didn't know where else to be. I think I went back in to sit and try to think all of this through. I honestly don't know. I've tried to watch the movie since, and I recognised the exact moment Mel called and felt instantly sick. I even bought it years later to try to defeat the moment in time, lay it to rest. It didn't work.

Comic Book Guy shushed me as I stumbled to my seat, and I reacted with utter fury. I wanted to smash him, to scream at him.

I felt my fist balling and my eyes bulging. 'Fuck you,' I said loudly, and he flinched in his seat and turned back to the screen.

I stared at the images, taking in nothing. I sat there for over an hour.

Far from my wife and daughter as they raced from Mullumbimby to Brisbane Hospital.

Far from my son.

Completely useless.

~

As I drove home from the cinema, my anger bulged. A man crossed the street far ahead of me, but it infuriated me. There was a pedestrian crossing twenty metres further down the road. Why wasn't he using that? Could he not see the risk he was taking? I accelerated towards him, infuriated at his lack of common sense.

Then I was home. With nothing that I could do. An empty home, just my footsteps. Waiting on the phone call to tell me what had happened. How bad things were.

~

Mel called from Brisbane. Third-degree burns to both hands. Mel's stepmother, Camilla, who was with them, called distraught and apologetic, snatching handfuls of blame from the air and trying to hold them.

'It's not your fault,' I said. 'Don't blame yourself.'

I was trying to swallow all the blame myself. I hadn't been there. Maybe if I had, it wouldn't have happened. Maybe if I'd not had asinine dreams of being a writer, I could have caught Tilda, stopped it all from happening.

It was my fault. It must be.

I wanted it to be. I wanted the pain to be mine. I wanted the fear to be mine. Instead, all I had was emptiness, punctuated by phone calls as people slowly started to hear the news. Mel's father. Her mother. My own phone call to England to tell my parents, straining to think what I could tell them beyond, 'Your perfect angry granddaughter is damaged now. Really badly damaged.'

I was so angry, and it was entirely focused inward.

I wanted my family home, wanted to hold them close.

~

My son arrived home a day later. Camilla flew him down and, along with my father-in-law, who had arrived as quickly as he could, we picked Sandy up. People were finding out about Tilda now. Word was spreading, and I still had no information, no vision of what had happened. Phone cameras were not a thing at that time, so I had no image of the damage. People were calling, though, constantly.

My son, three years old, rushed to meet me. He ran through the airport shouting, 'Dad,' and I held him so tightly. Camilla stood, looking exhausted, eyes clearly harrowed from having seen what I still hadn't. We hugged briefly before she flew back, and I tried to reassure her. It wasn't her fault. Things happen. It would be okay.

I had no concept of Tilda's injuries, just words.

Third and degree and burns.

Just words. They couldn't be as bad as they sounded. Three small words like that. They couldn't be.

I took Sandy home and, with my father-in-law, we watched *Finding Nemo* and *The Incredibles*, and I drank too much wine. Mel called to say she would be home in two days with Tilda, and for two days we entertained and spoilt Sandy, and life pretended to be normal, and I drank way too much wine, trying to muffle screams I had not heard and blot away images I had not seen.

~

At the airport, there they were.

My wife, exhausted – though, as we were soon to find out, it was possible to be far more than simply exhausted. And eighteen-month-old Tilda, two huge flippers over her hands. Bandages with tubes extending from them into which we had to drip water regularly to keep her skin moist. Tilda, wide-eyed and medicated with children's Panadol or children's Nurofen, one chasing the other every few hours.

We drove home uneasily, Mel so desperately tired, and me unable to grasp it. If we didn't speak of it, it couldn't be real, could it?

At home I took Tilda out in the pram, and Mel tried to sleep. I took Tilda to the park; she loved the swings. I thought, *I can do this, things can be normal, whatever is under those flippers is healing, bodies are amazing things after all. It's healing.* Maybe Grandad was right about faith-healing, maybe, if I focused on it, when we took the bandages away, we would see nothing but beautiful skin. Just like she had always had.

The benefit of a baby in huge bandages is you don't have to wait; other parents lift their kids free of the swings in a hurry and make way for you. I sat Tilda in and pushed her back and forward as she grinned, the pain medication doing its job.

Other parents, mothers primarily, came over to ask what had happened, what had happened to that poor girl, but all I could do was push. Backwards and forwards. They'd stand by me, nervously asking if I needed anything, if everything was okay, and I stood stupefied, seeing only my daughter and her huge bandages and smile, knowing the medication was ticking downwards to the point it would wear off and the pain from whatever was under there would rear up again like a shark from beneath still waters, all teeth and hunger and fury.

Tomorrow we were to go to Westmead Hospital. To the burns ward.

For now, I just stood, pushing the swing.

~

On the way to the hospital, an hour from our home, Tilda's medication wore off while we were caught in traffic. She went from quiet and resting to grisly and irritable and then to screaming, and screaming, and screaming.

We couldn't pull over; we couldn't do anything. We'd been told to give her the medication as she woke and then bring her in. Life was becoming so loud. Car horns and engines and Tilda bellowing in pain.

In the burns ward we were seen quickly. Ushered in, peppered with questions, given forms to sign. They explained debriding – the removal of dead tissue – and told us that that was what we would be doing today. We carried Tilda into a room with a bed, a screen mounted on the ceiling showing *Play School*, a woman whose job was to blow bubbles to keep Tilda as distracted as possible, a man with a mask who would keep the pain managed, and nurses – so many nurses – and us.

I watched them remove the bandages. The right hand was raw and red and wet and horrific. The left bandage came off and the hand was bloated, split, the arm burnt almost up to the inside of the elbow. She'd closed her left hand on the red-hot coals. Her right had stayed open. The left was worse. So much worse. The woman blew bubbles; the screen sang songs; the nurses removed dead skin, dead flesh; the pain guy did his job. Mel and I stood, useless, as Tilda's heart rate jumped higher and higher. At one moment she started to thrash and one of the nurses asked 'Dad' to hold her down. I realised that she meant me and leant forward, my hands on Tilda's shoulders as Tilda strained and fought against me.

'That's it, hold her still, please,' the nurse said, and I hated her, so very much. I wanted to lift Tilda and run, tear out of this room and never come back. As it was, I leant forward and used my weight to pin my daughter down as skin was snipped away and her right hand and forearm were laid bare to the world.

Tilda's eyes were rolling. Fixing on mine and looking away. Fixing and looking away. *Play School* was singing to us about the 'Bear in There'. I don't know how long we were in that room, but I find myself there often. Years later, I still find myself there. That horrific feeling of holding my child down as she was flayed.

After she was bandaged and we left the room, I held Tilda while Mel went to the bathroom. I imagined Mel went to weep, and I stood there, trying to be granite, trying to be British and stiff-upper-lip, firm with resolve and every cliché – but I couldn't. I pressed my face into Tilda's neck and gasped, shaking, and wept for a few moments, wiping my eyes on Tilda's shoulder.

She had an apple juice. They'd warned us that she might be sick as the anaesthesia wore off. The juice stayed down for a few minutes before she threw it up on the grass outside.

The following week we came back for more. More bubbles and *Play School* and tissue damage and scissors, and afterwards Tilda had an apple juice again. She frowned a few minutes later and, as I held her, I felt her control her breathing, still herself in my arms. The apple juice stayed down.

She was so tough, and so very angry. She'd lost one apple juice, and there was no way she was losing another.

~

In the days after Tilda got home, life became a fog. Tilda spent most of her time on Mel's lap, and Mel was in a constant state of jet lag. I'd play with Sandy and do what I could. Tilda studied her bandages, and they clearly made her angry.

Sitting on the floor one day surrounded by her toys, yet unable to pick them up, she pivoted and moved her foot. In front of her was a four-piece jigsaw puzzle, typical farmyard stuff – a horse, a sheep, a cow and a tractor. She frowned at it, and then put her foot on the horse. After a few moments, she picked up the puzzle piece between her toes and moved it to the other pieces – trying, failing, trying, failing – and then placing the horse in position.

She saw no triumph in it, she simply moved to the next tactile object and picked it up with her toes, slowly getting better at it. Crayons, wooden bricks, a book she wanted to be read, a soft toy, all were picked up by her undamaged and beautiful feet.

Since then, I've called her Toes. Those magical digits. Unable to use her hands, she quickly rewired herself to use her feet. Kids are remarkable and resilient.

~

We needed a skin graft on her hand but to achieve that we needed clearance from a cardiologist to confirm that there was no danger to her heart, with its ventricular septal defect. While Mel and her mum went to the cardio appointment, I took Sandy to the cinema, as we realised that he had almost been forgotten in this whirl of treatment and medication. We thought the news from the cardio would be fine. The paediatrician had told us not to worry, so this would be a check-box appointment, and then we could move on to the grafts.

Sandy and I chewed popcorn and watched nonsense and had an almost peaceful morning. Mel and her mother didn't.

The hole in the heart was likely small, we'd been told. It wasn't. It wasn't. It was large and in a dangerous position and would need open heart surgery. Not only would it need this surgery, it needed it as soon as possible.

I have a note from the time that I posted on Facebook. It says simply, 'I don't think I can do this ride anymore.' When Mel came home and told me the news, it seemed almost ridiculous. Like a screenwriter had come up with a lunatic idea for the plot. *What if, on top of third-degree burns, we throw in major heart surgery?*

Burns surgeries and open-heart surgery. I remember thinking that one day it would be years later. All this would be so far in the rear-view mirror that I'd be able to look at it all and feel okay. Feel like 'we got through that'. Writing this now, it's still not far enough away, even though it happened thirteen years ago. Writing this, it feels like it was yesterday; that constant plummeting feeling of *what next?*

We now had two insane circumstances. We were seeing the burns ward for the injury and seeing a heart surgeon as well. We were having

32

to tell the burns ward about the heart and the heart surgeon about the burns. He could see the bandages, so at least we had a head start there. The burns ward couldn't see the heart. Tilda was booked in for a skin graft – the first of several – and they sewed skin onto her palm: fifty-two stitches onto a palm barely bigger than a seashell. Fifty-two stitches that, post–heart surgery, would have to endure the hands swelling, as post-surgery hands can swell, as can feet.

Tilda was becoming used to anaesthesia. She never vomited, as she had the first time. She controlled her breathing and roused herself slowly. She would wake to find new dressings on her hands that she would look at, slowly flexing whatever digits were free to move. She'd sigh and sip juice, and we'd carry on. She knew about her hand, in whatever way an eighteen-month-old can comprehend such an injury, but she had no idea about her heart. She did know about her feet, though, and she continued to use them effectively, adjusting blankets and wrapping her toes around my fingers with what little grip she could manage.

The night before her heart surgery, I couldn't sleep. I stayed up in the lounge watching *Rage* on TV. They were playing a vast Led Zeppelin retrospective. I fucking hate Led Zeppelin. I don't think I did before, but I do now. Two hours of back-to-back Jimmy Page and Robert Plant in the time before Netflix and iPhones. Two hours where I was afraid of silence and measuring time purely by the changing flow of images, the ends of songs. Silence would have extended the night impossibly, a minute taking an hour, an hour seemingly lasting a full night. Led Zeppelin divided the time for me as I sat there, red-eyed and terrified.

~

In the morning we dressed Tilda, and she kissed her brother and her grandmother as we moved reluctantly, cautiously forward. Mel and I took her in to the hospital. I have no memory at all of the journey in.

We were name-checked and welcomed and ushered through. We found ourselves sitting in a ward where they gave Tilda a pre-op drug to make her compliant – almost drunkenly relaxed. She slowly became soupy in my arms, her gaze drifting around and her breathing deep and calm. Mel said she couldn't take Tilda through to be put to sleep. She was beyond exhausted by then. Tilda had only been sleeping on her lap for weeks now, which meant that Mel had only been sleeping sitting upright, holding Tilda in her arms. Exhaustion aside, Mel had seen so much by then, so much that I hadn't. The immediacy of the accident, the chaos of the ambulance and the flight. If she couldn't take Tilda in, then of course I could. Of course I should.

For the skin graft surgery, I'd taken Tilda through, and then trusted her to the surgeons after she was put to sleep. I'd dressed in scrubs and gloves and a mask then. This was to be the same, wasn't it?

Tilda was wheeled down, and the nurse was bright and reassuring. She made chitchat about how beautiful Tilda was and how much better she would be after the surgery. I was taken through, got dressed in the scrubs and mask, and came back looking ridiculous. Mel tried to smile at the sight of me all in blue – but couldn't. The nurse said it was time, and Mel tried to say anything – but couldn't. She reached out and touched Tilda's cheek instead. Then I wheeled Tilda into a room with six or seven people waiting. They were all there for Tilda, every one of them having a part to play in fixing my child, every one of them trained and dedicated and astonishing. But right then and there, every one of them was alien, unknown to me, and terrifying. A man in a mask stepped forward and explained that he would be putting Tilda to sleep. I nodded.

As Tilda saw the gas mask being lowered to her, she lifted her face upwards towards it. The nurses in the room fell quiet.

'I've never seen that before,' one of them said.

'She's had a few surgeries in the last few weeks,' I managed. Tilda's hands were in bandages.

As Tilda slipped under, a nurse said to me, 'Do you want to give her a kiss goodbye?'

For a moment then, I was completely convinced she would die. We'd been told one in a hundred children are born with a hole in their heart. Of those one in a hundred, it's only another one in a hundred that requires surgery. And only one in a hundred of those has complications. There wasn't a statistic for children needing heart surgery immediately after third-degree burns.

A kiss goodbye.

I couldn't. All the strength left me, and I sank to my knees, holding onto Tilda's upper arm as she fell asleep. It was the only thing keeping me tethered, stopping me drifting away, spinning upwards and outwards into space. I couldn't stand. I couldn't let her go. If she left me, she would die. I wouldn't have her back. She'd be lost in the hospital, in the system, between wards and floors. I couldn't let her go. I couldn't leave.

A hand touched my shoulder, and a nurse told me, 'We have her. I promise we'll take good care of her.'

'Please,' I said, struggling to my feet.

'We will,' she replied, and I looked down at my daughter. Fast asleep. About to go through doors for open heart surgery.

I managed to leave the room, and Mel looked to me for reassurance but all I could do was cry.

~

Many slow hours passed, and then we were allowed into Intensive Care. The surgeon came to find us and tell us all had gone well. They'd patched two holes, he said. Matilda was stable, and the surgery a success. We were led in to see her, an infant lying unconscious in a bed, tape across her forehead with numbers and letters on it, tubes in her nostrils and arms, nappy on, fat little legs limp. Tape and gauze on her chest. Machines pinging around her. Alive, asleep, beautiful and atrocious.

Mel photographed nearly every moment of our time in the hospital, and I heard her camera whir and click. The camera for her, in the hospital, slowed the things that were rushing by. I asked her later why she recorded everything, every moment, and she said she didn't know, but she felt that she should.

Tilda came round a while later. She blinked and saw us and rolled over and struggled upright and pointed to the door and said, 'Daddy, away.' She wanted out of there as much as we did, but she was literally tied to the bed with tubes.

Then she was on my lap under a blanket, asleep again. Then on Mel's lap asleep.

Beside us, a ten-year-old girl died four times in two days. Brought back to life over and again behind a curtain by the staff there. Her parents watched in agony as their daughter was cared for by hands not their own. We sat holding our girl and heard them sob, and then sit in stunned relief, then gasp and sob, and then again sit in stunned relief.

~

After a few days we were moved to a ward. Mel stayed at the hospital a few nights. I stayed one night. We got to know two parents who were there with their newborn. The baby had been born with leukemia, they explained to us, and they were facing a long road of tests and treatments and hours taking weeks and weeks taking months. 'I've never fed her,' the mother told us as she stepped behind a curtain to pump her breastmilk into a bottle.

On the evening that I stayed at the hospital, I went into the hall outside the ward and sat down on a wooden pallet and the father of the little baby with leukemia came and sat beside me. We swapped parent nightmare stories as his daughter and wife slept on in the ward behind us. We sat mostly in silence, but in a shared silence. A shared hope for each other's child. A shared appreciation for each other's pain. Five minutes away from the bedside and the bandages and things we couldn't change, couldn't fix. Five peaceful minutes before he said he should get back, and I said I should as well. He stood and then helped me up, put his hand on my shoulder and said goodnight.

A day later, Tilda was allowed to get up, and she toddler-walked to the toy room on the ward. I saw the other dad looking over at us, smiling. Then Tilda ambled to the hall. She looked at Mel and me, then at the length of the hallway, and then suddenly took off stumble-running.

Before the heart surgery, she'd go maybe twenty paces and then stop and rest her forehead on the ground to get blood to her head. We had never understood it before; kids are weird things and this was a quirk of Tilda's. But on this day Tilda stopped running after twenty paces only to turn and look back at us with a wide grin and take off again, her heart now doing what it was meant to do, unencumbered.

After a week, they let us go home. The dad of the baby with leukemia met us in the hall and held Tilda's finger and called her beautiful. He wished us well, and I shook his hand. So much of that time is a blur of best intentions, hospital sounds and utter fear. We left with Tilda, and those doors closed behind us, and it was only later that I realised I'd never taken his number or even learnt his name.

The simple silence of sitting with you, unnamed man, meant the world to me. I truly hope all went well for you, your wife and your daughter.

A Lasting Mark

Twice it came up during the run-up to Tilda's surgery. Two separate people asked me, 'What will you do if she doesn't make it?'

One of them was a work colleague who appeared at my desk after Tilda's accident with a cup of tea and a packet of biscuits. People like being told horror stories that they aren't involved in. They like to react in shock and horror, but from a seat of safety. She wanted all the detail, and to feel she'd helped by giving me a chocolate biscuit and a moment to cry. She sat on a chair she'd pulled over, and the first words to tumble out of her mouth were, 'Oh my God, Richard, I heard about your daughter's heart condition and the burns – what would you do if she dies?'

The conversation did not continue after that.

It wasn't the first lunatic thing that had been said to me. One of the managers said, 'She burnt herself? She must have screamed so much.' Another co-worker said, 'She could have burnt an eye out.' A neighbour offered, 'You must feel so guilty, having let this happen.' A mother in a supermarket said, 'Imagine if she had fallen face-first, my god, the damage! Can you imagine?' All of these things I hadn't imagined until someone else proposed them. Once they did, I could hear the screaming, I could see the eye gone, the face burnt, and I could grasp the guilt from thin air all around me for everything that had and had not happened.

The other time Tilda's death was mentioned was from a relative who retracted the question almost immediately, but it still hung there like a deflating helium balloon.

The idea became lodged in my mind, and I hated the hypothetical funeral director who would lay hands on my daughter. I hated him with a bitterness I cannot put into words. I hated the entire funeral industry for existing. I despised urns and coffins and death certificates. I could picture the jowly man with a click-top pen and clipboard sitting there taking details and offering me glib sympathy as he presented me with a bill. I despised him.

As Tilda grew well, the idea of her funeral receded, but the idea of the person who takes the information, who helps, who collects the deceased children from the hospital remained with me. A few years later, I took a redundancy package from work, and Mel told me to go for the job I wanted rather than one that would pay well – a decision we have only regretted a few times financially. Funeral work was all I could think of – the shadows of Tilda's time on the precipice feeling like something I was still beholden to. Her survival being something that I needed to earn.

During my first week in the first funeral home I worked in, I assisted in the dressing of a baby. Tiny fingers and feet. A cardigan. Socks. Booties. A woollen hat. Slowly, and under instruction, I put the clothes on the baby.

When baby funerals come, I put my hand up for them. I've sat with many parents now, and though I haven't been in their place, if they ask me, I tell them how close I came. I tell them about Tilda, and I recognise their pain. I can't compare my experience to where they are, but I have some comprehension.

Driving past the Sydney Children's Hospital, I can still feel it – the impotence, the slow crawl of time. I still flash on it all. A burnt body at work pulled me straight back to Tilda's injuries. Mel says I have PTSD, and I believe her, I absolutely do, but it's mine and I'm never letting it go. It's mine for not being able to stop the accident. For not being there when it happened.

~

Years later, in 2019, I was looking at Sandy and noticed his nose seemed off. Slightly swollen on one side. I noticed and then forgot. A week later I noticed again, and then forgot. A week later again I saw it, and this time I told Mel about it. She cocked his fourteen-year-old head from side to side and nodded. It was misshapen.

I eventually arranged an appointment with our GP, and she tilted her head from side to side, looking at Sandy's nose, and said, 'Yes,' and told us we would need to see an Ear Nose and Throat specialist. Then she said the word *tumour*, and it fell to the floor in front of us wetly, writhing and sick.

'Tumour?'

The doctor tried to reassure us, saying words like benign, but tumour pulsed there on the floor between us.

When Tilda had been in a bad way, everyone had known. Everyone was always calling for updates. Part of the exhaustion of that time was telling people the story and listening to their reactions. Calming their pain. As we came out from the doctor's, I asked Mel, 'Can we do this just us. No audience?'

As painful as it was for her, we did. Just us. Though she told her mum, I found out later. I don't think there is anything Mel's mother doesn't know.

An appointment led to a biopsy, and then to me returning to those same hospital rooms with a different child. It was now the time of Covid lockdowns, so only one parent could attend. My six-foot-tall fourteen-year-old had to attend the children's ward for surgery. Having his blood pressure taken by a nurse while he blushed furiously.

He was gowned up, and then asked by the surgeon if he had consented to the surgery. He looked at me confused.

'You're fourteen now, mate. You need to consent. I can't do it for you.'

Sandy frowned. 'I need this, though, right?'

I said yes.

'Okay, then,' he said and signed a fourteen-year-old's version of a signature.

Then I saw him settled to sleep, and then he was whisked away from me.

I sat in the waiting room thinking, *How the hell am I back here again?* For the duration of his surgery I was in a sustained panic attack. Heart hammering, breath hard to catch, nails digging into my palms.

Sandy woke up with his feet hanging off of the bed, huge boy that he was. We were in a room full of toddlers, babies and worried parents. His nose was bandaged, but he woke with the same soft smile he's had since he was a baby.

The surgeon came to see us a while later and said the biopsy had been successful, and that instead of taking a small sample, they had taken pretty much all of it. 'Now to determine what it is,' he said and left us.

'Dad?'

'Yes, beautiful boy?'

'I'm hungry.'

Knowing every vending machine in the hospital, I went hunting junk food.

~

We waited. For weeks. Waited, not knowing what word would be used. *Benign* or *malignant*. I was brittle again. Mel was as well. We were snappy with each other, with the kids, hiding in work, keeping busy. I hid my concerns in funerals and wine. Mel hid hers in work and long silences. The chaos of Covid in the hospitals led to delays in Sandy's results coming through. In front of Sandy, we remained calm. Out of his sight, we were fraught.

Finally came a phone call came from a very excited surgeon. What was in Sandy's nose was benign and evidently extremely rare. Some crazy cluster of cells that had connected in a blood supply and were happily creating a cell civilisation there. The hospital was having fun with the cells, they'd been discussing them in groups and writing about them. From our side, though, all we cared about was the word *benign*. It was all done. A brief stint back in hospitals with one of our kids.

Mel and I were both exhausted. Compared to Tilda, this had been easy. With Tilda in our past, though, it had been hard. Every corner was sharp, every doorway darkly ominous, every appointment threatening.

With joy we finally told the world that there was nothing to tell them – Sandy's weird nose was utterly benign.

~

When I had moved into funeral directing as a career, a young child came our way at the funeral home. Tilda overheard me talking about it to Mel at the kitchen table. She put all her soft toys into bags that night and told me to put them into the room where the child would be so that the child wouldn't be alone. Tilda was seven by then.

I arranged the room. Tilda's Big Ted watching over everything. I made the room as warm as I could, made a bed for the child rather than presenting them in a coffin. A pillow, a small mattress, a duvet.

The parents came and sat in the two chairs I had put by the bed. The mother picked up Tilda's Big Ted and held it tightly. She asked me if she could hold her child and I stepped in and lifted the soft and unforgettable weight of the infant into the mother's arms. She held her child and sang softly as her partner sat beside her, shattered.

I stepped out of the room, feeling my throat tighten with a swallowed sob. Tilda's Big Ted was pressed between a mother and her child, while the Tilda in my memory lay unconscious on the bed as she was taken through for surgery.

I've been in many rooms like that since, and I hope I am not the image I had of a funeral director – though I am getting ever older and developing jowls. I believe I am not the imaginary man I hated so much when Tilda swung uncomfortably close to death. I do have a black suit; I do drive a black car. I do have a phone filled with the numbers of hospitals, churches, clergy and celebrants. I hope, though, I hope I am not glib. I hope I don't offer shallow sentiments. Every baby I have cared for has been unique; I remember them all. Their parents I remember. They have all been calls I have not wanted to receive, but once they were with me, I wouldn't want anyone else caring for them. I collect the babies from the hospital, and I deliver them to the crematorium myself. I promise the parents it will be me at every step of the way. Then it is me who brings the ashes back to them.

One mother, months and months later, finally came in to collect her child. She saw the container and wept, and I held her. Time stops in those moments. Grief is a living and hungry thing that can swell to fill everything. It absolutely needs to be respected and allowed to live. It needs to be heard. At times it needs to dominate, shut us down and make us feel everything we would rather keep at bay. After sobbing for a while and drying her eyes, she left with her child, walking into the street holding the bag close to her chest as around her the world was its normal and unaware self.

On call one Friday night, my phone rang, and I moved to the kitchen, where I keep my pad and pen. I answered with the company name and my name. Speaking in a rush, a terrible flood, a woman told me her name and then said, 'I'm driving to be there when my grandchild dies.' She clicked off. My wife looked up at me and asked if I was okay, and I shook my head and then wept at the table. The clock was ticking, and a child was dying, and I was now a part of it too, and nothing could stop each minute from passing. While other people were out dining, dancing, driving, I was holding my phone and, somewhere in the city, the worst was happening.

I remember the fade away the world did when Tilda was diagnosed, when she was in surgery and after she came out. All I could hear was nurses' shoes squeaking and the monitors attached to Tilda purring and chiming. Nothing seemed to make any sound except whatever was immediately in front of me, of us. All I wanted to hear was my daughter's breathing. I still crouch by her some mornings, just to listen to her breathing. Children are such an incredible joy. They are stress and pain and guilt and exhaustion, but such joy.

The worst had happened for the family on the other end of the line. Now there was stillness and silence.

There is something correct about death in old age, a sprawl of memories left behind, spread like a quilt. There's something horribly understandable about dying, as my friend Chris did, far too young, from cancer. We've heard of cancer. We've seen it. It's comprehensible to outsiders, albeit never to the families. Cancer sinks its teeth in – but the word itself, we understand it. When we hear 'He died of cancer', we have a sense of it, because someone we know, or a friend of a friend, has battled cancer. It haunts the edges of everyone's stage. Car crashes, accidents, misadventure: they are terrible, but again we can imagine them, we can comprehend. It's a shock and an agony but we can still say 'he loved life' or 'she was such a warm person' because they lived every day up until that moment. They worked and laughed and ran and sang and did all the things we take for granted. They lived. They were loved.

Babies, they haven't lived. They've been loved from the moment they were known to be on the way, but they haven't formed memories, taken steps, watched *The Iron Giant* with their dad on Saturday morning while mum sleeps in. When babies die, I hear about it from the dads or from the partner who didn't carry the child. They phone, exhausted, and tell me over the phone that their son or daughter has been stillborn. They tell me the hospital has said that as it was over twenty-seven weeks' gestation they will need a funeral home. The word *cremation* falls from their mouths like cement.

For stillborns, cremation is the most common request. The crematoria do not charge for a child's cremation, and funeral homes keep costs as low as possible. Burial comes with unavoidable fees – the purchase of the grave, the formal coffin – and the moment of standing there over a hole in the ground, watching the coffin lower into the earth. For a stillborn baby, families often don't hold a formal service. The families I have worked with know the date and time of the cremation, and I encourage them to step outside, feel the air on their faces, hold hands, play a song, and quietly mark the moment somehow.

I meet them, and they are worn down. Eyes red. Tracksuit pants and stained T-shirts. Sometimes Mum comes with them. One woman, reduced to a sketch of herself, sat at my table and told me it was like Christmas had been cancelled after she'd seen all the gifts laid under the tree. She trembled as she told me the name her baby was to have. She held a soft toy and asked me to put it with her baby.

Dads or partners, they take on the responsibility for these arrangements. They try to shoulder the pain and move their mouths through the answers I need. They sign the documents I need them to sign, and I promise I'll pick up their son or daughter myself. I'll keep them informed, I'll let them know when I have a cremation date, I'll bring their child's ashes to them if they want me to, or they can stay safely with me until they are ready. Then they leave, telling me they are going away for a few weeks. Sometimes I don't hear back from them for months, their son's or daughter's ashes remaining on my desk in a small container, waiting for them to call.

Stillborn babies are astonishing to see. They are heartbreaking, yes, but removed as we are as funeral directors, they are also beautiful. They are haikus of a life unlived, often with a small woollen hat on their head and a blanket or shawl wrapped around them. I collect their paperwork from the social worker at the hospital, and they walk me to the room where the stillborns are held. I confirm the identity of the baby, then I lift them gently and place them in our carrier. I sign what I need to sign and leave the hospital as discreetly as I can.

One year, I looked after way too many babies. My signature appeared in the register too many times as I went back and back again. Each was unique, each was a dream started but unfinished. Each we arranged cremation for, and I then drove them to the crematorium and handed them to the staff member there, who took them quietly, each of us parents, each of us feeling their incredible weight.

One family, when I brought them the ashes of their child, took me to the nursery they had painted that now lay unoccupied. They asked me if their baby would have liked it. Was it right? Was it a good room? Outside, trees grew, cars drove and contractors jackhammered the road, but in this room, time was still. It was a perfect room; they were perfect parents. I hugged them both and left.

I hope children came their way. I hope their Christmas tree had gifts beneath it.

~

Other times – better times, I guess you could say – it is not the child that needs our help.

'Can you cremate a limb?' the hospital called to ask us.

'Well, yes.'

A child had lost a limb in an accident. The family wanted to keep the ashes. Could I collect and arrange cremation? I stood in the mortuary, feeling the small bag and knowing what was inside. I drove directly to the crematorium, the staff there flinching.

Awful, yes, but so much better a limb than a child.

~

Tilda was teased in school for the damage to her hand. Some kids called her 'Monster', and when I heard about it, I wanted to find the seven- or eight-year-old kids and berate them, find their parents and shout at them. I was livid. Tilda wasn't. She said that it was just those kids and their bad heads, and it didn't bother her.

The scars are a part of her and, as much as I hate their existence, I love all of her. She remembers the more recent hospital trips. The ones from her younger years are, thankfully, missing in her memory. She has met each trip with frustration, but also with intelligence, confidence, politeness and a deep appreciation for the nurses and doctors. Her fingers still wiggle, and she paints and draws and forgets to do homework, distracting me from her homework as well by baking apple pies.

She recently had her potentially last surgery: a scar release on the middle finger, which was curling inwards as she grew and the scar tissue did not. Mel and I took her in to the hospital for the surgery. The hospital was still on Covid alert, so only one parent could be with Tilda at any one time. We shuttled back and forth – my turn, Mel's turn – until the nurses said, 'There's no one in the waiting room at the moment, so you can both sit there.' We sat with Tilda, now fifteen years old, a full thirteen years and more since the accident. We were in the same room where we'd sat waiting all those years before, with the same TV playing the same kids' shows. When it came time for

Tilda to go through, we asked who she wanted to go with her, and she asked for Mum. Previously it had always been me who took her in to be anesthetised, and I'd come to see it as my role: Mel had seen the aftermath of the accident and I hadn't, so I should wear the ache of watching my child be put to sleep. This time, it was to be Mum.

They got up and walked towards the room, and I saw Mel collapse into a chair. Ahead of her was Tilda's retired burns surgeon, Dr Harvey. He'd been the calm voice throughout every appointment. The bowties and the colourful shirts and reassurance, with never a trace of accusation in his voice. Any time I have ever told anyone about Tilda's accident, I have expected them to say, 'How could you have let that happen?' because that is the question I have endlessly asked myself. But Dr Harvey simply dealt with what was in front of him. He'd retired a few years before and his sudden reappearance knocked my wife backwards.

Tilda looked back at me and said, 'Dad, Mum's crying.'

Covid being Covid, I stayed where I was, and Dr Harvey walked in and shook my hand and said warmly, 'Hello.'

A thousand words rushed up and fought to be heard. *Thank you. It's great to see you. God, you're amazing.* All I managed was 'Hi'.

He told me he'd come back in today to consult on a few surgeries and would be assisting with Tilda's. He smiled and left, and Mel took Tilda through.

Over lunch, Mel was quiet.

After a while she said, 'It's confronting, isn't it?'

Everything was. The hospital, the surgery, the memory. Everything.

A week later I was back for the follow-up. They took the plaster cast off Tilda and checked her over, and then put another cast on. They gave her an opiate for pain management, which led to her singing me the entirety of *The Rocky Horror Picture Show* in the car on the way back, in between telling me that 'It's all very okay, Dad, really very much *oooh-kay.*'

Another week later, and we went back again. The second cast was off, and Tilda was giving the nurses candy canes (it being the week before Christmas), while I sat quietly wondering if this was the last time we'd be here. Outside was a mother with her daughter. Severely burnt legs. Here for that debriding appointment. Covid meant Dad couldn't come through; he was outside on the chairs waiting, not seeing, not being able to help.

The nurses gave us silicone and Coband and dressings and talked me through aftercare – and then we were gone, heading home.

I didn't realise when I got home that I'd also brought along a big bag of tension. I became infuriated with Mel as I explained how to use the various dressings and she kept asking me questions. Everything fell on me and, after slamming doors and shouting and devolving into something basic, I ended up sobbing in a doorway, holding my daughter and saying I was sorry over and over. For everything, I guess. For every one of the appointments of the last thirteen years, every stitch and plaster cast and scar.

Grief has its way with you. You can't stop it. Even years later it is still there, neither friend nor foe, but as an essential. Waiting for the moment where it shuts you down for your own good and makes you sob all over again, letting off the pressure of the things you can't vocalise.

I do have PTSD, but as I said, it's mine, and I am keeping it. It guides me in my job every day.

First Funeral

It wasn't until I was forty that I reapplied for work in the death industry. It was 2013, and I'd clocked up twenty-odd years in jobs that were largely repetitive: clerical work, administrative oversight, part of a team following processes, and slowly getting older every day. Each day in those jobs felt like being in a holding pattern, waiting for clearance to land. Mondays were the same as Fridays were the same as March were the same as December.

As mentioned, I eventually took voluntary redundancy from the job I'd had since arriving in Australia. Suddenly being detached from routine was intimidating, and I spent a few weeks in a blur of eggs Benedict, books and school drop-offs, as I tried to work out what to do next. Mel told me to look for a job that made me happy rather than continue in the same corporate churn. She'd recently stepped out of her background in editing and moved into teaching English, as her mother had done.

'Do what makes you happy,' she said, and I frowned.

'I'm not sure what that is. IT training again?'

Most likely sipping a coffee, she shook her head. 'You talk about funerals a lot. Why not look into that?'

'It'll probably pay terribly.'

She shrugged, most likely drinking another coffee by now. 'We'll manage.'

Tilda's surgeries were still fresh in my mind – as I think they will be even if I make it to my nineties – and the whispered question of what I would have done had she died was still a sore tooth in my mouth. I was almost angry at the idea of the funeral industry, for being there waiting for people to die, lurking at the edges of the everyday world, biding their time until you were forced to walk over to them.

Despite my annoyance at the industry, I found that whenever I tried to think of the job that could make me happy, I pictured funerals. Not that I was going to swing in like a well-dressed Tarzan and change anything, but it seemed to me like a place where I would, or could, fit, even though I had no experience.

A temping agency offered me funeral work if I had a black suit. Fortunately, being forty, I no longer had a light (bright) green suit and *did* own something dark. I said I'd do it, and I drove fifty minutes to a cemetery, got there an hour early and waited for a hearse to arrive. When it did, I stood how I thought a funeral person should stand and saw the hearse driver nod at me. I walked over, and he thrust a clipboard at me.

'Take names,' he said.

I looked around.

'Those folk,' he said, with a jerk of his head. A small crowd of maybe fifteen people were standing by a little fountain.

I walked over and held the clipboard out. 'Could I take your names, please?' I didn't know what I was to do with their names.

One by one they took the sheet and signed, all of them far more familiar with what they were doing than I was. I walked back to the hearse and handed the driver the clipboard.

He ran an eye over it and grunted briefly. 'Good 'nuff,' he said.

From the passenger seat emerged another man, and a third walked over from a nearby car.

'Ready?' they asked me

'Sure,' I said.

The rear of the hearse opened, and they told me to stand on the right. The driver and the other man took the first set of handles and, as the coffin slid out, I took the next handles on my side. I felt the weight of the body inside as we stood. 'Thank you, gentleman,' one of the men behind me said, and we started to walk towards an open grave.

The group of people I had just taken the names of followed us. Two orange-clad gravediggers stood by the grave and, when we were close, they took the foot of the coffin from us and placed it on a bar over the grave.

'Okay, together,' they said, and the coffin was lifted by all of us again and settled on a second bar. Straps were quickly passed through the head and foot handles, and the diggers retreated.

A family member stepped forward and read a brief eulogy as rainclouds gathered overhead. Then she nodded at us.

The hearse driver lifted an old portable CD player that had seen far better days and pressed down hard on *Play*. Nat King Cole sang 'Unforgettable', and the three men walked to the grave and I followed. They each took a strap at their handle, and I took mine. A gravedigger appeared. They all lifted, so I did as well. The gravedigger took the bars away. The men started to lower, and I let the strap slip through my hand slowly as they passed hand over hand. I let it slip steadily, feeling it burn my skin, until the coffin settled at the bottom.

'Thanks,' the hearse driver said to me, and I realised I was dismissed. I turned and walked away and then drove another hour home.

I'd buried someone, and my palm had a red friction mark on it. None of the men had told me their names. I didn't know the name of the person in the coffin, wasn't even sure of the gender. I'd been too busy watching the three men for whatever cues I may need to follow, so that the eulogy had passed me by. None of them had given me any instruction at all, seemingly willing for me to bluff my way along. To watch and do as they did. When I work with new starters now, we work together slowly, we who are more experienced direct and repeat and lead the way.

That day felt unfinished, almost as though it hadn't really happened. I hadn't seen the grave filled in. I'd left a body in the ground, in a coffin that I'd carried. I'd looked down from the edge of the grave at the surface of the coffin receiving its last moments of sunlight. I'd smelt the wet of the cemetery soil. Seen the covered piles of earth and the shovels the diggers would use.

My hand hurt, and it was a long drive home, but I'd worked at a funeral, and it seemed to have gone okay. The hearse driver had nodded to me and said thanks.

A week or so later some money dropped into my account for four hours' work, and my wife asked, 'So, is that really the kind of work you want to do?'

And I said, 'Yes, I really think it is.'

Early Days

My first weeks in funerals, it was more than apparent how little I knew. I had expectations from *Six Feet Under* and every movie with dour men carrying caskets, but I soon realised it was nothing like 'November Rain' and Axl Rose. Nor was it the Dickensian quills and inkwells that I had half-hoped for – old leather-bound registers and files containing lives written longhand with due care. (I guess this turned out to be a good thing, as I am frequently told I have the worst handwriting in our office.)

Every day would commence with a Day Sheet showing what funerals were on and what each team member's roles were to be. After years of autonomous working in offices, it was strange to now have something like a school timetable to adhere to, but at the same time that timetable was a tremendous reassurance. Some days I would be trimming hedges (my first time was a disaster, as I cut through the power cord of the hedge trimmer), other days painting over graffiti on the side of the building.

One day I was being shown how the viewing room should look, candlelight, air conditioning, chairs in place, and my colleague opened the door and before us was an open coffin with a woman lying in it. She was still, silent, neatly dressed, hair set, and eyes closed.

'Are you okay?' my colleague asked as I was obviously silent, and I nodded. 'That's the first body I've seen,' I said. She gasped. She apologised, asked again if I was okay and I said I was, I was fine. I don't know how I expected to feel or what I expected to see but the lady there in the coffin was peaceful, still someone's mother or grandmother but only in shape now. The lights were out. The power switched off.

Some days, if things were quiet, I'd be listed to spend the entire day in our chapel, scrubbing and vacuuming and polishing. I spent the day cleaning the dust from the wooden ceiling, cleaning the windows and doors, and touching up paintwork on fences on the roof garden. I am far from good with a hammer or paintbrush, but this tactile ownership of the environment dug in a confidence and pride in the building itself. It made it feel like my chapel, my building, my responsibility.

A colleague spent a morning showing me how to wash the vehicles. Hose them down, then a bucket of warm sudsy water and a sponge all over the car, then rinse, then chamois, then scrub the hub caps and shine the tyres, then the insides – vacuum and polish the dashboard. Everything clean, petrol tanks checked – as soon as they nudged half a tank we'd refill. Branded cars were only ever taken to the service station by someone in a shirt and tie. At all times, it was drummed into me, we were on display. If you are driving a hearse, people see you; if you are in a branded car with the word 'Funerals' on it, then people notice. Hearses drive slower and take the route of least lane changes and turns. Headlights on. You don't want to glance over and see a hearse driver beating the steering wheel singing heavy metal songs, picking their nose or eating a meat pie. If a hearse cut you off in traffic, it's pretty certain that you'd notice the name of the funeral home and hold it in some disdain. Come the day you needed assistance, you'd shy away from calling that number.

From the moment we leave the building in uniform we are on display and, as taught, we move slower, we react slower, we speak slower and, essentially, we drive slower. You'll never hear a hearse sound a horn.

Lasting impressions are also a consideration. With every location we attend, we strive to ensure that we are always welcome back. This covers hospices, nursing homes, churches, doctors' surgeries, crematoria, cemeteries: we are only ever as good as our last interaction. It was drilled into me from my first funerals to only speak if I was certain as to what I was saying. I was told again and again to be polite, to be respectful, and, although it sounds like common sense, having it reinforced over and over again made it second nature to double down on presentation and communication. We can't function without all the people we are dealing with across the industry, and good relations with them are essential.

~

I was taken on a transfer early on by a colleague. Two of us would always go on a transfer; two sets of hands were needed for lifting and safe manoeuvring. We drove quite a way out of the city to a smaller nursing home. The children of the deceased were still there when we arrived. I'd handled maybe fifteen transfers by then, but this was my first with family still in attendance. My colleague was leading the interaction, and I stood respectfully back and waited for the moment when we would need to move the lady into a body bag.

My colleague spoke with the family and introduced himself and me. The family were clearly reluctant to leave.

'We do need to place her into a body bag,' he said, and their faces dropped. 'Now, you are welcome to stay, nothing untoward is going to happen, but it can be a confronting final image, to see a parent in a body bag. If you feel you would be okay, then I am quite comfortable with you staying.'

They looked uncertain.

'Or,' he continued, 'you can help us. You can help us lift and place her; you can see that she's safely with us.'

The daughter looked at him. 'We can do that?'

'Only if you would like to.'

She looked at her brother and said she wanted to. He nodded and said he would help too and, from there, step by step, they helped us lift the woman's body while we slid the bag beneath her, and then settled the body into it, the daughter placing in flowers and a soft toy, the son slowly kissing her head.

'We need to seal the bag now,' my colleague said, and the son looked at the zipper.

'Can I?' he asked, and we nodded.

Gently he pulled the zip upwards, bending to kiss his mother again before closing the bag over her face and hugging his sister. We slid the body bag onto the trolley and left.

'I didn't know we could do that,' I said, when we were back in the wagon.

My colleague nodded and said it wasn't normal but sometimes you could see that a family needs to be involved. Sometimes it helps them to do the final steps. Whatever we can do to ease the pressure and provide reassurance we should do.

Now, if I'm on a transfer, it's my colleague's voice I can hear, long after he retired, and it's a variant of his words I use. If people want to be involved, we involve them.

~

We used to conduct transfers all hours of the night. If it was your week on call, that meant it was your week covering the after-hours transfers as well as working your day shift. My first week on call was hard. Adjusting to that 'anytime, anywhere' feeling. The phone would go, and then it would be suit, shirt, tie, shoes and to the car.

One morning at barely 2am in a local nursing home, a colleague and I lifted a woman gently from her bed towards the trolley and body bag. Her mouth, close to my ear, exhaled a long and slow sigh. It's not something you can ever become used to, and I froze as the hairs on the back of my neck prickled and flashes of text from Henry James and Bram Stoker came to mind in this dark bedroom.

'She's said goodbye to you,' my colleague said. 'Come on now, let's go.'

The nurse outside watched us go, smiling as we moved back outside into the cool of the night and she resumed her shift.

~

During my first burials, I stood where I was placed and did exactly what I was told. Somehow, no matter how heavy the coffin, we always managed to reach the grave. Carrying a coffin with rope handles over a lengthy expanse of grass, weaving around existing graves, I would feel the rope gouging into my hand. By the time we reached the grave I would always have a livid red welt across my soft, office-worker palm.

Once, we found ourselves carrying a coffin through a cemetery in heavy rain, with lightning flashing down around us, followed by swift thunder. When we reached the grave, the ground was slick and churned. As usual, the gravediggers received us and took the foot of the coffin to lift it to the bearer bars. We followed their lead, awkwardly hefting the coffin in order to raise and move it further across the bars. Before we could slip the straps through the head and foot handles, the side lip of the grave gave way, and the earth slid, taking one of my colleagues, Peter, with it – or one of his legs. Peter cried out, 'Oh my goodness!' and we looked up to see him suddenly splay-legged – one foot in the grave, quite literally.

The family around us gasped as we helped him back up. He ran his hand up and down his legs, and we waited for him to find a tear in fabric, a tear in skin, even a jut of bone. Fortunately, there was none, and Peter stood and clapped the dirt off his hands as thunder boomed again and we continued with the interment.

Later, Peter came back from the doctors with the best medical note I have ever seen – *injuries consistent with falling into a grave.*

~

I stood in the back of many a Catholic church, lighting the coals for the thurible. I would blow on them gently to spread the red heat, hear the sizzle, and then swing the chain to keep the air flowing and the coals glowing. I spent time in the back rooms of the churches, where the communion wine is stored, where the candles await their turn, out of sight and away from the funeral for a few moments. I learnt where this church kept the coals, where they kept the matches, learnt to try to have a lighter on you anyway, for the times when you couldn't find the matches. I learnt where to leave the thurible after the service. I used to have a notebook. I'd draw bad diagrams of church layouts, driveways, scratch down notes on where the light switches were, should I need them. All the things that, after a few visits, you just know anyway. These days, I can return to a church I haven't been to in years and the back of my mind finds the file and pushes it forwards with everything I need to know.

~

I remember on one occasion standing, again, with Peter. The minister stumbled, and the thurible came open, the hot coals falling to the floor of the church. In an instant, Peter knelt and scooped them up bare-handed, gently but swiftly tossing them back into the vessel and standing, as though nothing whatsoever had happened.

'Good grief!' said the priest, looking at Peter's hand.

'It's all fine, Father, please continue.' Peter, unflappable.

I'm yet to develop asbestos hands.

~

During the first funeral I ever conducted, Peter saved me. We'd parked outside the church, and I was a whirl of nervous energy. I knew the family, I knew the service, I knew the church, I'd booked the cars: I was really doing this. I was a funeral director. That phrase still fills me with pride, all these years later. I deeply love and respect what I do for a living. That day, though, I was still green and was trying to do everything at once. I had the rear of the hearse open and had removed the gooseneck that keeps the coffin in place.

Usually, at the point when we remove the gooseneck, we place a metal pin in to keep the coffin secure. I didn't, and I stepped away, unaware that the coffin was starting to do what gravity would have it do: to slide towards the lip of the hearse with a steadily increasing speed, from there tumble towards the floor, and from there towards bad publicity and a family who would never forget their father's coffin, shattered on the road because the conductor hadn't placed the pin in the hearse when he removed the gooseneck.

We are only ever as good as our most recent funeral. I think every funeral director knows that.

On the steps, Peter came up to me and nodded to the hearse. 'I put the pin in for you – coffin would slip out on a hill like this.'

I looked and saw what he meant, saw what could have been.

'Shit, thank you.'

'No worries, Rich,' he said and walked back to the memorial book. Unflappable, eyes on everything. Everyone needs a Peter.

~

On rare occasions, we would recieve a repatriation to Australia. The deceased person would be flown from far overseas. Arriving in a shipping crate, in which was a cardboard packing box, in which was a coffin, in which was a metal liner. We would pick them up from the airport, which meant wrestling safety vests over our suits and then reversing the hearse into the airport loading bay. A forklift would appear, carrying our container. It was slid gently onto the deck, and we then lifted it, with help, onto the rear rollers of the hearse. The windows of the hearse were blacked out and we drove the crate slowly back to base.

Once back, we had to open the liner to re-encoffin the body for the church service. We opened the liner with tin snips, like a giant can of beans.

I remember one time, at this stage, making two snips, three, and then suddenly the smell hitting us in a wave: dank and meaty and cloying.

The body, which should have been embalmed, was poorly preserved. With each cut through the metal, more and more was revealed of the wet and confronting flesh within. My stomach didn't roll, my gorge didn't rise: I was just somewhat in awe of what the body could become. How, when the lights go out and the engine turns off, we decay – naturally breaking down, layer by layer.

The smell, though, was there in the back of my nose for days.

~

I sat in on arrangement meetings when I first started. I was the spare wheel in the corner, listening, watching, learning. I sat in on five meetings within a week, and each was filled with loss and love. Families whose mother or father had suddenly died, or passed after long illness. There were tears, smiles, coffees were drunk, papers signed, and ice broken between the arranger and the family. This was the essential part, the first few moments when you have to win your family over, reassure them that you can do what they want and need you to do. I watched my colleagues, how they did it with such grace, and hoped I would find my own way.

I was initially tongue-tied when it came to starting off these meetings. You can't be crass or artificial. You can't be overwhelming or exaggerated. During those early meetings, finding my voice instead of impersonating my colleagues was hard. I wanted to do things *right* but I didn't yet know how to do things *well*.

It's easier now, being older, greyer, a little more lived in. It's easier now, knowing my churches and cemeteries and crematoriums, my religions and traditions. It's easier now that I have a phone full of rabbis and reverends and priests and celebrants. It's easier with all the tools to hand – but the meetings are never simple.

~

A few weeks in, a client came through the door without an appointment, and everyone else was busy. I was asked if I thought I could do it, and I jumped up, keen to help. I met the family in the room, had my file and pen, and expected the same love, loss and tears as I had seen in the weeks prior.

Instead, they were icy. Furious. They had despised their dead relative. They had no wish for anything more than to be rid of them. Every answer was flecked with rust and fury. Every moment of the meeting was one they could hardly abide, still having to talk about this person who was now gone, and thankfully so for them.

As they left, I was uneasy. In my naivety it had never occurred to me that the deceased could be someone unloved, unwanted.

I described the way it had gone to my colleagues, and it came as no surprise. 'That's a bit rough for your first one,' I was told. Suddenly I had a new understanding – a strong sense that this is one of the ways it can be for us. We aren't all loved and lamented.

'Do they want the jewellery back?' I was asked.

I shook my head. 'They don't even want the ashes.'

Usually, people come to me with their love stories: how and when they met their husband; the life they had with him; the favourite song of their wife, and when they danced to it; the memories of their father swimming, singing, smoking or driving; their mother, painting, or calling them every day. They speak about the deceased in the present tense, and then catch themselves.

It's so rare that people come to us as my first family did, with anything less than love for the deceased, that it becomes unforgettable when they do.

A man told me outside the chapel one day that he hated the deceased. 'I'm about to go in and be nice in the eulogy, but I hated him. I just want someone to know that.' He sucked on his cigarette and looked inside. Then he nodded at me, went in, and his eulogy had most of the crowd in tears.

~

The first ever phone call I made as a funeral director came after we received a message that ashes had been found at a tip. Ashes from a crematorium have the name of the facility at the top and then the funeral home at the bottom. The person who had found the container looked us up and phoned through. They gave us the name of the deceased, and we looked them up.

'The ashes were thrown away?' I asked, trying to imagine how that could happen. Being new to the job, the ashes seemed as sacred to me as the deceased.

'Looks like,' said my colleague. He sat back and steepled his fingers and then looked at me. 'Why don't you call the family and see what they want to do?'

'What do I say?'

He frowned and then said, 'I have absolutely no idea. See what you can think of.'

I sat, the phone on the desk like a coiled snake ready to lunge, and tried to work out what to say. I dialled the number slowly but soon enough it was ringing and soon enough a voice at the end said, 'Hello.'

'Hi, this is Richard,' I said, naming the funeral home. 'I'm sorry to disturb you.'

'Okay,' the voice said.

'We've had some ashes come back to us that were found at the tip. I'm just calling to see if we can return them to you if this was an accident.'

'Nah, mate,' said the voice.

'Of course. So, would you like us to arrange for them to be scattered somewhere? Is there anything we can do for you?'

There was a beat of silence and then, 'Do whatever you want.' Then the line went dead.

~

On one of my first trips to the coroners, Peter and I were collecting a larger person. The coroners are wonderfully respectful and capable people, working seven days a week, twenty-four hours a day. The bodies that go to them are people who pass away at home with no doctor able to attend to provide a cause of death, or people who die in more unfortunate circumstances. Part of one of the documents we complete before cremation asks if we suspect any item on an Agatha

Christie–type checklist has happened in relation to the deceased: violence, poison, abuse or neglect, drowning, suffocation, burns and others. If the answer is yes to any of these, then the deceased should really move to the coroner. The coroner is there to rule out foul play and confirm, for us, that a funeral can go ahead. While disinterment is possible later on, it would never be possible to un-cremate someone.

On this day, the coroners had done their ruling out and we signed the person out without any hitches. We confirmed the belongings that came with them, and then wheeled the heavy trolley out and rolled it into the lifter, to be summoned from the lower floor where we had the car.

We went down and reversed our car so it was backed up to the doors of the lifter, then pressed the button to bring the trolley down. The lifter settled, we removed the safety chain and we pulled the trolley towards us. Being inexperienced and less able, I slipped, and the trolley came shooting out too fast. The gentleman was secure and safe, but the trolley wheel came down on my right foot – hard, and *very* heavy.

We caught the trolley and set things right and recovered.

Peter said, 'You okay there, Rich?'

'Yeah. Yeah, sure,' I wheezed, limping to the car.

'You sure now?' he asked, as we squirted hand sanitiser onto our hands. Funeral directors found the shift to sanitiser during the pandemic quite simple, given how frequently we used the stuff anyway.

'Yeah, no, yeah.' My foot was screaming, but I was okay I said.

Driving back, I thought something was amiss – but I could stoically grit my way through it, I was sure. I limped as we unloaded the body. I limped up the stairs. I limped as the boss asked me why

I was limping. I made excuses for the limping, and limped through the next few days. I was two weeks into the job and didn't want to tarnish myself with an entry in the accident book already. I wanted to be quietly capable, not clumsy and injured. I limped through funerals and limped through hearse-washing and, finally, a few weeks later, my wife insisted I go to Emergency.

Emergency for an injury from several weeks before. I felt ridiculous as I explained to the nurse that I'd dropped something heavy on my foot.

'What was it, sir?' the nurse asked me.

'The wheel of a trolley.'

'And what was on the trolley, sir?'

My foot was several shades of purple and grey.

'Uhm, just a few boxes.'

'Was this a workplace injury?'

I was stupidly afraid of saying yes to that question.

'Only you have a hairline fracture of your foot, which is likely causing you some pain.'

'Will it heal up okay?' I asked the nurse.

The nurse raised her eyebrow.

'You'd be best staying off it as much as you can. It needs time.'

'Okay, thanks, that's great,' I said and basically fled.

Of course, it would have been okay if I told work about the injury, but at the time, new to a job I really wanted and was fast falling in love with, I did not want to be a sore thumb sticking out with my stupidity.

I limped through the next few weeks and got it into my head that calcium supplements would help me recover. As it is, years later, I feel like one of those old fellas in books and movies who can feel a storm coming. If my foot tingles, aye, there'll be a hard rain coming.

~

On the day before one of my first rostered days off, I was helping to lower a heavy coffin into the ground. We all focused our attention, letting the straps move steadily and evenly through our hands, and letting out a small breath of relief when we felt the coffin safely touch the ground. The family around the grave tossed in earth and then turned and took their first steps away from the deceased, towards whatever tomorrow may be for them after the wake.

'That was a heavy one,' I said to my colleagues. I think I felt it more than they did, still being fresh from office work and sitting all day long.

The next day I had to take Tilda for a check-up. On the way we stopped at the laundrette to drop some wet clothes off for drying. Lifting the basket from the back of the car, my back suddenly screamed. Everything locked up. Somehow, I got the laundry inside and inched back to the car. Tilda, pleased with a day off school, was chattering away in the back seat as I drove, wincing.

I was nosing along Botany Road when the car made a loud and concerning cracking sound and smoke started to billow from under the hood. I pulled into a side street, my back still hurting and the car fast dying. At the side of the road, illegally parked but without a choice, I called for a tow, and then took Tilda to the doctor. My back was slicing pain through me and Tilda, realising that I was struggling, placed herself under my right hand and put my hand on her head.

The doctor gave her the all-clear, and we left, the tow company saying they would be an hour. I bought painkillers from a supermarket, and we went into a cafe to await the towers. Tilda devoured milkshakes and chips, and I swallowed one, two, three and then more painkillers. I was desperate to lie down; time moved slowly.

The truck came, and we watched our car being taken off to be humanely destroyed, then called a cab and waited by the roadside. Tilda was quite delighted with the chaos and adventure. In the back of my head, I knew I needed to keep moving, to work out the kink in my back, but all I wanted was to lie still and be fed soup through a straw.

These days, if we are burying, I know better how to stand. How to hold the ropes. How to balance myself. The weights we carry are the definition of unusual. Short distances often, but, once lifted, we can't drop them. We know this. Lowering a coffin six feet into a grave can be a long distance to cover slowly. But a coffin can't be allowed to thud into its final rest.

So we do everything slowly and with care. If there's pain, then it comes later, and we deal with it later.

Chris

One of the problems with being a funeral director is people say, quite often, 'Ah well, one day you can bury me.'

My mother-in-law has said it over Christmas lunch – although she's my mother-in-law, so in her case I do say, 'It'll be a genuine pleasure.' Friends have said it at dinner and started listing left-field requirements – naked viewings (of which I have done one – the deceased naked, not myself), live music, a magician, a spring-loaded coffin (so they can leap out to a loud cry of *Tada!* at their own funeral). Can I put marijuana in the coffin so they can get the crematorium high? Can ashes really be put into vibrators? The boss at the funeral home has made it very clear how she wants her funeral to happen – shoulder-carry, horse and cart, all the pomp and all the ceremony.

All these familiar faces telling me that when they die, they want me to look after them.

Another problem is that, once you've seen a certain number of dead bodies, it is easy, frighteningly easy, to picture any person talking to you as a body on a stainless-steel tray. That person there on the bus, or serving you coffee, or chatting to you in a meeting: cold and lifeless, the internal lights all off, the animation gone, lips slightly parted, eyes closed – or waxy, unfocused and wide open. Skin pale, framed by a body bag or a fallen mop of hair. The cold butcher smell of their bodies, which I have found to be like uncooked lamb shanks.

Then there are other smells that come with the dead. Along with the unfortunate but apparent meat smell, there is the deep smell of the last breath slipping out from their lungs or the thick fetor of the last gas escape from the bowel – honestly, a final fart is unlike anything you've ever known. Then there are less common smells: the wet, green-smelling stench of decay for those found later, sometimes very much later; the clutching and insistent smell of a body found in water. A scent that almost daubs itself onto you, into you.

Then there are the faces of the dead. Some are shocked, as though caught in a moment of revelation as they died, one last crossword clue solution on their lips, or some major piece of news that would have stopped the show had it been heard. Some are serene, perfectly comfortable with their ending. Some appear almost amused, a tug to their lips, as though they were about to whisper a punchline or finish a great anecdote. Some seem disappointed, almost irritated to be dead – cheated at a final hand of cards. Those are the ones I imagine who wanted to see their own funeral, to see who wept and who laughed and who only came for the free sandwiches and champagne.

~

I got a message from my friend Chris one morning. 'Hey mate, I think I need to see you soon.'

Chris had cancer, but he was fighting it. Well, we all made ourselves believe he was, in the way that we say, 'Ah, he's a fighter,' and hope that somehow there is a way he can glove up and punch the cancer back.

People said of Tilda, when she was injured, that she was very brave. I remember snapping at one person that no, she wasn't. She had no choice but to go through this. There was no bravery, there was simple fact: *she has to endure this*. The person I snapped at looked crestfallen and confused. They were pre-programmed to say of any sick child they heard about 'Oh, she's brave' and then to walk away believing that the pain was somehow lessened by this imagined tenacity.

Chris was fighting it, because that's what it made us more comfortable to say. He was a fighter. He was getting treatment. He was young. He was cool. He'd make it through.

Actually, he'd told me he wouldn't. He'd already told me it was terminal. But I was selfish. He was my friend, I loved him, so he would make it. He'd fight because I hoped, and because so many other people hoped.

'Professionally?' I messaged back.

After a few minutes, he replied. 'Yeah, sorry, hope that's okay.'

~

I'd stalked my way into my friendship with Chris. I first saw him years before I ever spoke to him. He was up on stage with almost the entire cast of *Mad Max* running a Q&A at my local cinema. *Mad Max* I liked; movie trivia I loved; seeing things on the big screen I'd only ever seen small I very much liked. Mel and I were waiting for the movie to start, and this ball of energy came rushing onto the stage to a packed Randwick Ritz crowd, clutching a microphone and grinning enthusiastically. He launched into childhood memories of smashing cars on the sidewalk and the thrill of watching *Mad Max* at way too young an age, and I thought, *He'd be fun to talk movies with.*

I started going to more of his events. Sometimes with Mel, and sometimes with friends. After a screening of the Michael Caine movie *Harry Brown* with a live link-up to the director in the UK, I saw Chris wander by as I waited for my bus home. Sharp boots, leather jacket, cigarette in his mouth. I thought, *Go on, ask him for a smoke, tell him you loved the screening*, but instead I looked down at the floor and said nothing, and he wandered by in a cloud of cologne and smoke.

I think the only time I ever jumped over my basic shyness was when I saw George Miller, the director of *Mad Max*, ahead of me in a cafe in Bondi one day. He was buying red velvet cake and going shockingly unrecognised. I stood fidgeting and promising myself I wouldn't say 'Are you George Miller?' until the person ahead of me left and I was directly behind him. As he turned to go, I said in a rush, 'Excuse me, but you're George Miller?' He smiled. In a rush I thanked him for *Mad Max* and called the recently released *Fury Road* a bit of a dream come true. He laughed and said it really was, for him especially, and he shook my hand and left. I was massively overwhelmed. Each year since, Facebook still reminds me of the moment that 'I JUST MET GEORGE MILLER'.

When Chris walked past me at the Bondi bus stop, I didn't quite have the confidence I had when I saw George Miller. Chris chastised me for that years later. 'Why the fuck didn't you just say hello?' he asked. 'We could have drunk more beer.'

As advice for life goes, you could do worse than 'If something great is in front of you, say hello to it'. You'll get to have more beer and more good times.

~

Chris ran caption contests for free tickets to hype the screenings he arranged. Turns out I am not too bad at putting captions under pictures of Ray Winston or Quentin Tarantino. The first thing I won was a Blu-ray of *Django Unchained* (which meant I had to go and buy a Blu-ray player). Then I won tickets to see *The Sweeney*, then opening-night premier tickets for *Jurassic World*. My son's eyes almost popped out of his head when he saw the free popcorn and pizza and the packed cinema and giant countdown on screen to the 'Opening of The Park'. Sandy, in the cinema, looked around at the hundreds of packed seats and said, 'Does the man who gave you the tickets know all of these people?' Then the dinosaurs came on, and we were a father and son watching a T-rex, and the world was in good pizza-fed order.

After five or six wins, Chris messaged me: 'You're a funny fucker'. We started talking on Messenger. About the screenings. About music. About life.

Chris was cool. Knew everyone. Knew every band. Knew every director. And he was fascinated with my job. One afternoon I got a message from him saying he was zeroing in on his next screening and asking what I was doing.

'Just left a meeting with a with a one-legged man about his deceased sister,' I wrote back.

'That's just not normal,' he replied, and then said he'd been shut in all day.

This was after maybe a year of chatting online. I was ridiculously like a kid with a crush.

Nervously I typed, 'Then let's have a beer.'

The message balls bubbled, and he wrote, 'Okay, where?'

As mentioned, my self-confidence is never high. I know I am good on the phone. One of the office workers at a Jewish synagogue I liaise with often used to say to me, in her Irish accent, 'Ah, Richard, read me the weather report, I love your voice.' A few weeks later I was at the synagogue, and I went upstairs to meet people there, and the Irish woman looked up at me and said, 'Ah wow, genuinely a face for radio. You're totally not how I pictured you.' To this day that remains the most eviscerating comment I've ever received, though thankfully she was smiling. I've told families since, though, when they compliment my voice, that I am the definition of a face for radio.

That day, presented with the certainty of actually meeting Chris for the first time instead of chatting online, I was awkward and uneasy. So far, I had only been text in a bubble to Chris. Captions under photographs.

The casual clothes in my locker at work weren't cool. My trainers were falling apart. My deodorant was cheap chemist's stuff. I kept reminding myself I was in my forties and meeting someone for a beer, not attending a job interview, but that feeling of not being cool enough, good enough, just wouldn't shake. With every passing moment I felt more of a schlub.

I'm a social smoker, and I knew Chris was a copious smoker, so I bought a packet on the way to the pub. I walked in and saw him sitting in the smoking area with a beer in front of him and cigarette curling smoke from the ashtray. I walked over, and he looked up, grinned hugely and stood up.

'The man himself,' he said and clasped my hand.

And it was easy. Conversation was easy, smoking was easy, drinking was easy. It felt like I'd known him forever. The simple, utter pleasure of making a friend happens less as we get older, but damn it is wonderful when it occurs. For those four or five hours in the pub, conversation never stopped.

Come time to leave, he gave me a huge hug and said, 'Let's do this again soon.'

And we did. And then again, and again.

One time, meeting Chris at another pub, I wandered in early and some random lad from Essex on his backpacker Australian holiday shouted, 'Look! It's a fat dad.' I felt immediately deflated and texted Chris to change pubs, not wanting to sit there alone with red cheeks smouldering as I deliberated on whether I really was a Fat Dad. Chris said that was fine and we met across town.

'Why the change?' Chris asked when he got there.

I told him about the Fat Dad heckle. I thought it was quite funny, now I was away from it – the red-faced slap of the moment was behind me, and it was mine to retell as an anecdote rather than a humiliation.

'Fuckers,' he said.

A few minutes later, a blonde girl wearing not a lot came over and asked us for a light.

Chris and I had been mid laughter about who knows what, and Chris handed her his lighter without looking her way as we carried on chatting.

'Thanks,' she said. Then added, 'It's so nice.'

Chris, taking a sip of drink, asked, 'What is?'

She blew smoke and said, 'You two. Able to be out and in love.'

Chris exploded in laughter. 'Jesus,' he said. 'We're not gay.'

She went red and asked if we were sure, maybe expecting this to be the moment where we both realised we'd been living a lie.

'Pretty sure.'

She seemed genuinely disappointed and left us.

'I love you, man,' Chris said and started laughing again.

'Hey, I love me too,' I said.

'I love you, Fat Dad,' he said, and raised his glass.

~

He messaged me one day: 'Hey mate, you're coming to see The Cure with me tomorrow.'

I barely knew The Cure. I said there'd be people who'd likely enjoy the gig way more than me.

'Maybe, but I want to go with you.'

We drank for several hours in Surry Hills, I ate a crab burger (which was the best David-Cronenberg-looking meal I have ever had) and then we arrived at the gig. For three hours The Cure were excellent, and I was on a learning curve. I didn't know three-quarters of the songs, but they were tight, exhilarating and confident. After the gig, Chris had arranged a car. It dropped him at home first.

As he climbed out, he said, 'Next time come over to my place for whisky.' He nodded to his waterside apartment.

I said sure I would.

Unfortunately, I didn't make it there until after he died.

~

After he said he had to see me professionally, I went to visit him in his ward at St Vincent's Hospital. He was smaller, his cheekbones pushing outward. Instead of a leather jacket and boots, he was wearing a hospital gown. He still had his smile, though, and still had his vocal swagger. He was charming the staff at the hospital and for a while we just caught up, chatting the same old nonsense but without the beer.

After a bit, he nodded to my bag. 'Got your work stuff?'

I pulled out the file. We worked through the questions one by one. I learnt his middle name was Vaughn, which sounded appropriately cool. He wanted to be cremated, he said, no fuss. Then a big send-off at Jangling Jacks on Victoria Street in Potts Point afterwards. He has his name on the bar there, right on the corner at one of the best spots.

'You'll pick me up, won't you?' he asked, and then apologised. 'Sorry, man, that's fucked up. I shouldn't ask that.'

'No, it's okay. I'll pick you up,' I said. 'But that's a long way off.'

Chris smiled and looked down at his hands. 'Yeah, I don't think so.'

Then, in a 'fuck death' moment, he smiled and said, 'Let's go have a smoke.'

We went down in the elevator, talking about the ridiculous idea that had just been mentioned in the media of Quentin Tarantino directing a *Star Trek* movie. Then we sat outside St Vincent's and smoked two in a row each. I recognised funeral directors pulling in for paperwork before they drove around to the rear of the hospital and the mortuary.

We enjoyed the sun and the slow tick of time, and then Chris said, 'You're cool, you know. Fuck the fuckers who don't realise that,' and he shook my hand, and we hugged. Then he walked back into the hospital and waved goodbye from the door.

~

His partner, Charlie, called me early one morning not long afterwards. Chris had died at Sacred Heart Hospice during the night, she said. Mel and the kids were away, and Christmas was fast approaching. I was due to go up to my in-laws' house on the Central Coast that night to deliver the bikes we had bought the kids for Christmas, which the kids utterly believed they weren't getting. Two new mountain bikes needed to be delivered: proper dad duties in the run-up to tinsel and mince pies.

I told Charlie I would take care of him. Then I called the hospital from work and said my friend's name instead of the name of a stranger. They told me Chris was ready for collection, and I said I'd be on my way. One of my colleagues offered to go for me – but I'd promised him I'd collect him myself.

In the mortuary, he was there. Yes, I had pictured this moment, hoping that by imagining it I could ensure that it never happened. He was cold. The pure energy of his animation now gone. We wear gloves on transfers every time, but I took mine off and touched his cheek. The mortuary attendant looked at me with eyebrows raised.

'He's a good friend of mine,' I said, and the attendant nodded.

'I'm sorry for your loss,' he said, and I zipped Chris's body bag closed.

That night, Chris safely in our mortuary, I drove the bikes to my in-laws' house. My father-in-law gave me a beer and said he had heard about my friend. He asked if I needed anything, and I said, 'I think I need to get a bit drunk.' He smiled at me and said that would be okay. He brought up a bottle of wine from downstairs, and we drank, talking about friends. By the time my mother-in-law got back from Rotary, I was several sheets to the wind – enough that she left me a note in the kitchen that I found the next morning, ordering me not to drive back to work unless I was sure I was sober.

~

A few days later, Charlie met me at work. I had the hearse parked out the front with Chris in the back in his simple coffin. Behind Charlie were her mother, Julie-Ann, and Chris's father, Colin. Charlie hugged me, and I shook hands with Colin and Julie-Ann.

It was a bright-blue Bondi day. I explained that Charlie would ride with me in the hearse, and they would follow behind. We'd pull over at the cortege line of Macquarie Park Crematorium, and I'd be able to open the back of the hearse for them to have a few minutes with the coffin, but I reminded them that it had been Chris's wish that he have no funeral at all. No eulogies. No prayers. Just this small moment. Charlie would come on with me to the back of the crematorium for us to deliver Chris.

We played Bowie on the way there, and The Black Angels. At the cortege line, Colin touched his son's simple coffin and said, 'I have been so very proud to be your father.' As Charlie and I delivered Chris, the gentleman at the delivery door stood respectfully and wished Charlie well. They received Chris tenderly, and by the time we were leaving, he was being cremated.

That afternoon, we drank, and we missed Chris. Over the next few weeks, I grieved harder than I had realised I would. My wife and kids were still away and, one whisky-couched night, I booked a tattoo of the logo of Chris's company (PROM – the People's Republic of Movies). The tattoo turned out larger than I was expecting, and I worry now about the day when I am too old to remember what PROM stands for. I haven't reached that day yet. These days, when I am asked, 'What does your tattoo mean?' I like telling them about Chris. My friend.

One evening, a quiet post-Christmas night when Mel and the kids were back, we were watching *The Shawshank Redemption*. Morgan Freeman delivered the line about missing his friend, and I started to cry. My son and daughter saw me, and I imagine, for kids, seeing a parent cry is both disturbing and strangely magical. Parents don't cry, and if they do, then something big must have happened. Parents work and clean and read and drink (too much) wine. My son came over to me, closely followed by my daughter, and they sat either side of me for the minutes that I needed to cry, each resting their heads on my shoulders.

It is different when the funeral is for someone you know and love. I know that. I know that for every person coming through the front door it is different. For them it *is* a person that they know and love. I try to never lose sight of that.

~

Chris told me to write a book one day and make it cool. After all, if it's not cool, is it really worth doing?

I said I'd try.

He shook his head and said, 'Nah, you're cool. You'll manage it.'

Darkness

'On call' means up at any hour. One week in every five, the funeral home phones are patched through to my mobile, and for those seven nights I am on call, while continuing my regular work during the day. It used to be one week in four. Now it's one in five. The worst I ever had it was one week on in every three and that was an unsustainable insanity.

My kids have learnt that 'on call' means that when Dad's phone rings they lower the volume on anything they are doing. Tilda did an impression of me at the dinner table a few years back. She imitated my phone voice, 'This is Richard, how can I help?' It was eerily accurate until she said, 'Who's dead, and where are they, dammit?'

For years we would physically complete all after-hours transfers ourselves, irrespective of the time of night. This was before our staff numbers reduced and we didn't have the capacity to crew things. Now we use the services of a trusted outside provider that specialises in deceased transfers. It wasn't unusual to be up at 2am in a shirt and tie, boot heels clicking on the street as I walked to my car to collect my offsider and head out to a residence or nursing home. Hospitals can hold people; they have mortuaries. Nursing homes do not.

We do get asked, though: 'How long can Dad stay here with us?'

The simple answer is that we move when you tell us. If you don't want us to leave yet, then we don't. Once you say go, we'll be there within two hours, depending on traffic and where we are when you call.

'Can Dad stay overnight?'

As long as the doctor has been, yes. But, gently, I explain to the family that things will happen. Dad will likely pee his last pee, or perhaps pass a final bowel movement. A little movement or jostling can make things move along. The dead can break wind, they can sigh, they can moan or growl as whatever is left within them finds its way out.

~

One man called at 4pm and asked us to come not before 9pm to collect his partner. He sounded tired but calm; the death had been long expected, and they were okay, he said. I assured him we'd be there by around 9.15.

We arrived at a beautiful home hidden away down a side street off a side street, away from the noise and crowds, in amongst trees and soft street lighting. We were met by dozens of people drinking champagne, a television playing pictures of the deceased, and music, bright and upbeat and beautiful. 'We're having the wake,' they told us.

The deceased lay in bed surrounded by candles and friends, pet cat sitting on his legs. Beside him was a medical cause of death issued by the doctor.

I explained what we needed to do, the body bag requirement, and they stepped back and let us prepare. Gently we slid the deceased from his bed onto our trolley, and as we went to close the bag, the cat leapt in, which caused an uproar of laughter. The cat curled up and lay on his chest, peering out at us calmly.

'He wants to go along too,' someone said.

The cat gave us such a look. A look of complete understanding. The chest he had lain on so often before was still. The breathing sounds he had heard so many times were gone. The warmth from the body was cooling.

'C'mon, puss,' we said gently, and the cat stood, stretched, looked at his owner one more time and stepped from the body bag like a Disney Siamese, all grace and curves.

I was relieved. I'd been asked before by the family of an elderly person, 'If we have the dog put down today, can it go in the coffin with them?' I'd said no. The deceased was going into a vault, and I explained the need to embalm. There couldn't be a dog in the coffin as well. The eldest child nodded and said, 'I reckon we can have the dog in an urn by next week – can you put that in with them?'

That night, after we closed the bag, we turned to see that the deceased's friends had placed their glasses down and had formed a guard of honour from us to the front door. As we moved the trolley, it passed from us to them along the line, being lifted at the stairs and moved out into the street as we followed. Hand by hand, lovingly, along and upward. Outside, they walked with us to the wagon all holding hands, smiling.

The trolley slid into the wagon, and we drove away, all of them waving us off and the cat standing on the wall outside the home arching his back in the night, watching us go.

~

Dark streets. Silent streets. But not always.

One night, I was pulling out of the work car park after midnight, driving on my own. A man in a white doctor's gown was running down the middle of the road. What looked to be blood was splashed all over his coat. He was howling and, on seeing my headlights wash across the road, he turned and ran directly at me.

I saw behind him a cluster of others in white coats. Medical students partying after graduating, I guessed. The guy running at me was wild-eyed, way past intoxicated, screaming 'MOTHERFUCKER' and waving what I hoped was a fake scalpel.

I swerved around him, and the clutch of brand-new doctors all started running towards me as well, a swarm of white gowns and medical chaos chasing a mortuary ambulance. There is an irony there somewhere.

This is how the world ends, I remember thinking. Drunk zombie doctors.

~

Headlights splashing like milk into black coffee. Turn left, turn right, left again, and the lights wash over the car-struck body of a cat. The red brake lights of a car ahead flash before swinging left and disappearing. I swerve around the cat, and the night goes back to darkness again.

I feel upset about the pet, maybe more than I feel about the dead grandparent waiting for me at the end of this trip. Every time I tap the brakes, I see the creature again. Dead only seconds before I turned.

A family at home not yet knowing their cat was gone. A street of trees soon to have 'Missing Cat' posters put up on them.

~

Another night, I am sitting outside the roller doors downstairs at the funeral home, blinking and yawning and waiting on a body to come in from another crew. The bushes ahead of me part. My car, parked next to me, is silent, the engine off and headlights off; the only light comes from the faint green of the emergency exit sign and the distant electrical sheen of the city.

A fox nudges its way out through the bushes and sniffs the air. It blinks and looks up at me, holds my gaze for a few moments. Beautiful wide eyes and soft orange fur. It steps out into the night, long tail twitching behind it, feet stepping lightly. I crouch by the roller door and watch it watch me.

'It's okay,' I say softly.

It steps intimately into the night, sniffing the air and seeing me as no threat. It walks slowly towards me, and I briefly hope I can stroke its neck or ear. Instead, as it sniffs the air, the van I am waiting for comes around the bend and throws light along the alley.

I glance up at the van, and when I look back, the fox is gone.

~

Parking near home one night, or as near as I can get, I swing the car door closed and it makes a loud, creaking groan. I frown; it hasn't done that before. Then it groans again, louder and longer. I stand looking at the car, confused, before pennies drop in my late-night brain, and I realise I am hearing sex. Late night, post-pub, post-club, windows open, the hell with the neighbours, overcrowded city sex. I walk away as moans bounce off brick walls and tumble down the street.

Turning the corner onto my road, I walk past another open window, from which I hear a man saying, over and over, 'Will you just fucking die. Will you just fucking die. For fuck's sake.' I hope he's playing a video game.

~

Another night, just pushing 1am, I'm less lucky with parking and have to walk quite a long way home from the only space I can find. The ocean crashes softly in the distance, and my shoes click-clack on the concrete. I can see three girls ahead, see them looking nervously my way. I am tired, I want my bed, but I know what I look like at night. Black trousers, black boots, black shirt. I look like every slasher movie ever made. The man-shape walking closer, closer still. I am Michael Myers. Jason Voorhees.

The Funeral Director: my own horror movie.

Tired as I am, I stop and let the girls walk further from me. I can see them still glancing at the now stationary man-shape behind them, the shape now malevolently standing under a lamppost watching them.

I can't win, really; I am creepy either way.

I give up and walk home as they quicken their pace ahead of me.

~

Quietly, we stand over the deceased in a bedroom. The family wait in the living room. We lift their mother into her body bag. A long, deep sigh slips from the lips of the deceased.

The last breath of ninety-seven years, the last sound, a gently musical note that only I hear.

~

I sit waiting on a van, parked in the darkness under a tree. I watch the end of *The Good, the Bad and the Ugly* on my phone for perhaps the hundredth time. I'm watching Tuco sprint across the cemetery as, outside the van, the street sleeps. Then I realise it isn't all asleep. An older man is walking, and he stops outside a house as a security light comes on. For half a second, he and the house create the perfect image of *The Exorcist* poster: Father Merrin coming to attend to Regan, and I almost clap in delight.

One simple post-midnight moment that no one would ever believe.

Then he walks inside, and I go back to watching the gun fighters gather, seeking Arch Stanton's grave, and to waiting for the van.

~

The phone rings, around 2.30am.

'This is Richard.'

I can hear breathing. Long, slow inhalations.

'Can I help you, my friend?'

Breathing only.

I remember a colleague told me about a man who called to report his own suicide. He'd said he was killing himself and asked us to come in around an hour or so. My colleague snapped, calling him selfish. He told the caller to think about the damage he was doing, think about the people who had to listen to this – how did he think it felt to hear someone say they were killing themselves? How was this fair to the person at the end of the phone line? Had he stopped to think about anything beyond himself? Stop it, phone for help. The caller rang off. Hopefully he didn't go through with it.

This night, I listen to the breathing, I wonder if this is my turn. A suicide calling me in the act.

'Do you need help, my friend?' I ask again, and after a few moments, I hear a man's voice.

'Where's my father?'

I flick through the day; I know we brought a man into care.

'What's Dad's name?'

Breathing. 'What the hell kind of fucking question is that?'

'One I don't know the answer to. If you let me know his name, I'll be able to tell you if I know where he is.'

Breathing. Then a version of a name.

'He's with us. He came into our care this afternoon.'

'Fuck's sake.'

'He's safely with us.'

The breathing.

'We'll give you a call tomorrow.' I read him the number from the first call sheet.

'That's my number.'

'I know.'

'How'd you fucking get it?'

'The nursing home gave it to us,' I say, addressing him by name, which causes him to hang up. I am left in the dark at one end of a broken call, with him at the other end, I imagine blinking blearily.

Weeks later, I stop at the man's home with his father's ashes. I walked past a gate hanging off one hinge and knock on a screen door. I hear a clatter inside and call out my name and who I am. I knock again and peer into the darkness. Suddenly I see a man rushing towards the door, blasting it open with a kick. I step back as the man erupts, one fist swinging. He turns to me, one fist upraised still.

I hold up the ashes. 'Your father,' I say.

He blinks.

I hand him the clipboard and ask him to sign. He slashes the pen across the page.

He takes the bag, peering into it.

'Your father,' I say again, and he looks at me, blinking as I leave.

~

I'm just back from a transfer forty-five minutes from base. It's 3am, and it's not worth going back to sleep now. I'm normally up at 5am and it takes me an age to fall asleep. The slam of the back of the car is louder than it would be during the day. The creak of the driver's seat. The guttural chug of the engine. It's all so loud.

The phone rings. It's a call from the same place we have just come from. A different ward. Another death. Forty-five minutes to get there, twenty minutes to do the transfer, another forty-five to get to work, fifteen to unload and write the details in the mortuary book, and then fifteen minutes to get home. Two hours twenty minutes at least.

People are sleeping soundly as we pull back into the night.

~

It's just kissing sunrise, and I'm bleary from a 4am call. The sand on the beach is beginning to glow as the sun rises. Down there are early-morning joggers and the tractor combing sand clean.

I park by the shore and walk to the baker. I buy one of the first batch of croissants, fresh out of the oven, and a juice.

I sit on the bench in my black suit and eat as, around me, the suburb wakes. I'm due at work in two hours.

Faith

My grandad, Cyril, really did think he was to be the next Jesus. I wish that was a lie and am very aware it sounds like the start of a John Irving novel, but I'm afraid it's true. He showed me his palm when I was eleven and pointed to the way the lines crossed.

'Can't you see?'

I couldn't. I could only see an older man's hand.

'The lines, they make a cross. A perfect cross.'

They didn't, but in his eyes they did. I saw the normal lines on any palm, whereas he saw a cross and, as he traced with the index finger of the other hand, there was an outline of Jesus as well.

This perfect cross and fuzzy Jesus meant that he would be coming back as God's son. 'I have achieved the perfect level of love for all humanity,' he told me. 'I've learnt the lessons and worked through the wheel of star signs. I am ready.'

He gave me limited advice during his life. He told me that, since he had experienced being drunk during World War Two, in the stores of some far-off army base where he was stationed, that I should never drink. If I wanted to know what it was like to be drunk, I could call him and ask – there was no need to ever try a drop. He also told me that the police could always see me, no matter where I was, which led to an anxious childhood believing entirely that a policewoman was watching my every move on a curved old cathode ray television, making notes of any transgressions. He told me, when I was thirteen, that I had limitless powers and gave me a bright orange paperback book called *Your Powers and How to Use Them*. This book gave step by step instructions for astral travel, communication with the dead, mindreading, faith-healing and other sexy and less-than-sexy X-Men powers. I tried reading it, but I remained disappointingly power-free. Grandad also advised me once that 'everyone has blood in their stool one time or another, don't panic about it'.

My mum told me once that Weetabix were spider eggs and you had to eat them quickly, otherwise they would hatch in your bowl, so I'm guessing this kind of thing is genetic and that my kids will one day relate back to me the semi-insane things I have said to them.

Grandad called my mother daily after my parents split up. Part of this communication was to relay his deep disappointment that Mum was now a single mother and therefore a blight on society. It was also to keep up his telling of his lifetime of faith-healing successes. He'd saved the souls of an entire platoon of soldiers from World War Two one evening when he'd found them lost in London. He guided them all towards the light via the basement below his unit. His description of it was evocative – kitbags and boots, marching constantly, until they bumped into 'Old Cyril', and he guided them homeward through an old concrete wall to heaven.

His war diaries had him in the middle of every major moment and had him calming a squad of Australian soldiers by singing to them during a conflict. The diaries ended with the words: 'After the war I married and had two children. The End.'

~

Cyril was a man who was never wrong and who had an opinion on everything. After I moved out of home to move in with a girlfriend, he wrote a Christmas card to me that read, 'I can't believe you have left your mother. You're as dreadful a man as your bastard of a father.'

I had already written his card and sealed the envelope but, after reading his message to me, I scrawled on the back of his, 'Lovely to get your message, Grandad. Stay the fuck out of my life.'

We didn't speak for a long time after that. We met again at my uncle's sixtieth birthday party, where, when asked if he had any children other than my Uncle Steve, Cyril replied, while sitting right beside my mother, 'Oh no, I only have the one.' He'd still not forgiven Mum for being a single mother.

His recorded eulogy to himself was complimentary of himself and of his storied and heroic life. Of his spiritualism and his faith-healing he spoke at length. He'd told me at various times that he had cured cancer with his bare hands, healed livers, and had my liver removed by a blue orb alien and washed in gold liquid to cure the hepatitis that I never had. He told me once that he 'healed a black' and that this proved he was the next coming of Jesus, as he had demonstrated before God his love for 'all of God's creatures'. I guess we all narrate our stories to make ourselves sound better than we are. I am more than likely guilty of the same in this book.

I am sure somewhere in there was a good man, but I didn't meet that version.

When I was nudging my teens, Cyril called to speak with me. He ran me swiftly through his latest psychic understanding, as provided to him by his guides. I was not Richard Gosling, I was Eddie Setchell. Eddie was his brother and had died young of a burst appendix, the fault of a drunk doctor, according to family legend. Cyril had a paint-by-numbers picture I had done terribly, and he'd stood it on his fireplace beside a picture of Eddie. Three nights in a row, the painting had fallen from the fireplace, and on the third night Grandad had understood finally that I was Eddie.

'How does it feel, being called Eddie?' he asked me.

'Uhm,' I replied.

'It will take some getting used to, but you are Eddie. You aren't Richard.'

'Oh,' I managed.

'Soon we will take you and have your name changed. You're my brother, and it's time we let this Richard business go.'

Mum took the phone, and I wandered to my room, not knowing if I could be forced to have my name changed or how I would broach this with my dad. Then I thought, *Why would I even bring it up? There's no way this is happening.*

Mum came up to see me a little later and asked me how I felt – was I okay with this news that I was Eddie? With a sickening lurch, I realised that my mother seemed to be accepting it as fact as well, and I now had two people pushing the Eddie idea.

'I don't think I am Eddie,' I said, trying to be diplomatic but knowing absolutely that I was NOT my dead great-uncle.

Mum nodded and then said, 'I know, I know it's hard. But maybe a change of name might be a good thing?'

Richard is not a great name. My brother-in-law spent years trying to make Dicko a thing when I first got to Australia. It is my name, though, and I'm pretty used to it. During life, I have occasionally tried to insist that my name is McQuint and to portray myself as rugged, capable and cheroot-smoking. My sister-in-law gave Sandy a T-shirt when he was a baby that read 'Son of McQuint'. McQuint was cool, Eddie far less so.

The phone trilled downstairs. 'That's Grandad again. He said he'd call back after we had time to talk. Would you like to speak to him?'

I shook my head.

'I think believing that you may be Eddie has brought him peace. He loved his brother.'

'I'm not Eddie,' I said.

I then had my one great moment of pre-teen James Dean, John Hughes rebellion. I said as firmly as I could, 'I am not Eddie. I'm me.'

My mother said simply, 'Oh.'

~

During the Eddie epoch, Cyril insisted to my mother that I be brought to his church. Cyril was feeding Mum money (which she desperately needed), and I guess he made it clear the money would decrease were I not to attend.

We went to London, and it turned out that his church was a small, sweaty hall. There was a slight rise at one end, a series of chairs like an AA meeting and polystyrene cups for weak tea. The room was half-full of elderly people, who were all looking at Cyril like he genuinely was Jesus. They doted on him, listened to him, and he laid his hands on their arthritis and head pain with a wide smile. He greeted my mother warmly and introduced me as Eddie. I said my name was Richard.

'It's okay, Eddie. I've explained.'

'Richard,' I said again.

'Eddie can read auras,' Cyril said, and I was ushered up onto the minimal stage. An elderly lady sat before me, smiling, waiting for me to tell her what colours of the rainbow surrounded her.

Rheumy eyes watched me. Cyril was staring sternly. Mum sat willing me to say anything. I had confidence enough to state that I wasn't Eddie, but to flee the room, to sprint into the streets of London and tumble into whatever tragic adventure that may bring – I didn't have that fortitude.

'Uhm. Around her head, I see yellow,' I said, seeing nothing around her head beyond a blue rinse haircut.

'CORRECT,' boomed Cyril. 'The yellow represents her warmth and bright spirit.'

'And ... uhm ... around her arms, I see red.'

'CORRECT,' he boomed again. 'The red shows her pain from the arthritis.'

I rattled off colours and was correct every time. I almost said tartan at one point just to see what would happen.

I diagnosed migraines, gout, eye problems, lung issues, all by declaring a colour somewhere that I could not see. 'CORRECT,' Cyril would shout, and by the end, I was applauded. As I stepped down, an old man handed me orange cordial and a single digestive biscuit.

These people gave thanks, they said amen, they had unwavering faith in Cyril (and digestive biscuits) and they believed that I could do what he said I could, simply because he had said it. I knew the opposite to be true. I couldn't see auras, and I absolutely wasn't Eddie.

This was belief.

~

We sang hymns in school by rote, never thinking about the words. We never questioned what balm was, or why Jerusalem was builded instead of built. We just sang them, and then said the Lord's Prayer, and that was that. Church was for weddings, and funerals.

When I became a funeral director, I was an atheist, and I still am. I prayed as a child every day at school, and one Sunday I was preparing to give thanks for Mum's Sunday roast, when my dad stopped me. 'That's just for school, mate,' he said.

I think the only time I ever felt religious was at Christmas, but that wore off. I was in the nativity – well, in the choir anyway. I never made it far enough to be a Wise Man. 'Little Donkey' and 'Silent Night' and 'We Three Kings' all had a Pavlovian magic about them. Sing the songs and Christmas gets closer and it was more and more real that Jesus had been a baby away in some far-flung manger.

I say to families, if they ask my faith, that I'm an atheist who goes to church every day. I'm Jewish on Monday and Catholic on Tuesday. Anglican Wednesday. Sometimes I'm Greek Orthodox as well. Buddhist. I've been Anglican and Catholic in the same day. Jewish and Uniting on the same morning. Had a funeral service with a stand-up comedian, a Catholic priest and a Buddhist monk attending.

A woman said to me during an arrangement meeting one day, 'And are you Catholic?'

I said I wasn't.

'Then how can you arrange a Catholic funeral?'

'Well, I'm not Jewish but I can look after our Jewish clients. I'm not Anglican but I know and understand and respect their traditions. I'm not Uniting but I have good relations with the Uniting ministers and can support any funerals needed. And no, I'm not Catholic, but I know all our local priests and understand the traditions that make up a funeral mass.'

She wasn't happy, but her sister hushed her, and we moved on.

I didn't know how I would take to religion being so ever-present in funerals. I originally had my pre-conceived idea of the Catholics and Anglicans and Jewish. All based on nothing more than my not believing what they believed.

Within a few days of starting in funerals, I saw a minister at a crematorium giving blessings and a committal. I watched people following along, saying amen. Then I was in a church learning how to light the thurible. 'This Father likes the coals to be white-hot before you go up. Make sure they are white-white-hot.' Then I was speaking with rabbis and reverends and finding a staunch humanity in them all, a great will to care and comfort.

My job is largely to care and comfort as well, and I've found, from tiny church to cathedral, the clergy always have a vein of care running through them. A warmth and softness of voice and an ability to bring ease after the worst has already happened.

~

We have looked after the Jewish chevra kadisha for over a hundred years at work. During Shabbat, we take their phones and arrange the transfers of their deceased. This was a wide world of mystery to me when I started. My manager at the time told me that if I was delivering a deceased person to the chevra, I would be recorded visually and with audio. 'Don't you swear in the chevra,' he told me. 'They'll know.'

Consequently, when my colleague and I first transferred the deceased to the chevra, we used to do it silently, just in case. We communicated by nods and simple gestures. Later, of course, I found this to be nonsense: there were no cameras or microphones. I still find that I do things silently when I am at the chevra, though.

A Jewish funeral arrangement was also a thing of mystery to me. We look after Jewish cremation, or burial in unconsecrated ground, but by the time I had completed many Catholic and Anglican services I was still unsure what to do for Jewish ones.

A colleague said to me, 'It's simple, there's no coffin choice as they use the plain black with rope handles, and there's no flowers or music. The downside is, it's quick.' It really is. Jewish burial happens within twenty-four hours of death, a little longer if you pass away on the Friday night Shabbat. Cremation is almost as swift, and, given the unpredictable nature of funerals, taking on a Jewish case can mean suddenly having three days' work to do in one, while still managing the other funerals on your desk.

I started meeting rabbis and found their humour and intelligence wonderful to be around. I hadn't known until then that rabbi meant 'teacher'. It took time, but slowly, steadily, the rabbis shifted from being professional colleagues to being people I thought of as friends.

When Chris died, I was in a bleak place. My mind felt like it had shrunk, and I was struggling with the memory of his body, his face with the smile no longer in place. I had thought I was okay – that I would be okay – but I kept returning to the Chris that was no longer around, the messages that weren't coming in anymore, the beers that weren't being pulled and the movies undiscussed.

On top of that, my uncle Steve had just passed away. The kids and I had made a whirlwind trip to England to see him after his diagnosis of oesophageal cancer. Steve was six-foot-nine and had a voice that bubbled up from somewhere beneath the Earth's crust. Up until I was thirteen, he used to hold me upside down, one-handed, and laugh as my face turned red. He had by far the foulest mouth and had endless stories. As a limo driver, he'd driven Madonna, Ed Sheeran and many others. He'd met Mike Tyson, sung 'Swing Low' at Prince Harry's request and, possibly or possibly not, cleaned the Kray twins' cars as a boy. Every story about Steve was too big to believe, but somehow utterly plausible. In the few days we managed to spend with him, my kids fell in love with him, and he hid his illness from them. But I'd see him each evening, sitting in the back garden, wrapped in a blanket and staring at the moonlight as time ticked way too fast.

With these two deaths coming so close together, I was struggling and, besides leaning on my wife and my kids and sporadically and quietly crying as I drove from work to arrangement meetings, I ended up speaking with two of the clergy I worked with often.

One was a Catholic. I'd conducted many funerals with him in recent years and had been quite in awe of his ability to deliver the service tailored each time to the youngest attendees in the room. If he saw one six- or seven-year-old, the whole ritual would change shape, and he'd deliver it almost entirely to them, with everyone else charmed and reassured by this almost bedtime story experience. He'd helped me out with services where I knew children would be in attendance who'd lost fathers or mothers, and come the end we'd both been exhausted but the funeral would have been cathartic.

'Are you okay, Richard?' he asked me, around the time I was struggling with these deaths.

I shook my head. 'You know, I think I'm not.' I told him about Chris, and about Uncle Steve. 'Two of the finest men I've ever known.'

He smiled at me and put his hand on my elbow. 'I'm sorry to hear that,' he said, and then reached into his pocket and pulled out a tin of mints. He shook the tin open and asked me to pick one and hold it. He took one himself and then said, 'Now give me your mint and I'll give you mine, and you'll feel better. Mine is a gift to you, and yours is a gift to me, and gifts from friends are blessings.'

I took his mint, and he took mine, and the funeral soon began. I did my part with mint-fresh breath, and he did his with grace and poise.

When it came time for the final blessing and incensing of the coffin, he walked around splashing holy water and then, facing me, splashed me copiously.

He said to the crowd, 'A little extra for our funeral director today, who's grieving his own loss.'

Strangely, I felt lighter. Calmer.

Wetter, but better.

As we wheeled the coffin out, I felt one of the family place a hand on my back, and before we left, the widow hugged me and said I hadn't mentioned anything and should have done. 'After all you told me about not holding grief in or keeping a lid on things.'

A day or so later I was at the synagogue and the rabbi asked me the same question. 'Are you okay, Richard? You seem quieter.'

Again, I explained. I'd lost a dear friend, and then lost a dear uncle very quickly afterwards.

'A friend? That is a terrible thing to lose. And then an uncle straight afterwards? Richard, one death is bad, but two, two is so clumsy.'

He smiled at me, and I felt myself grin.

'Smiling is how we honour love. We are gifted with friends and family and should smile about them as much as we can. Tell me their names?'

'My friend Chris, and my uncle Steve.'

'Chris and Steve. Good men, friends and family to a good man. You'll be okay, Richard.'

Then he took the box cutter he used at each service to cut the garments of the bereaved and slid the blade forward. He held it down towards my groin and said, 'Remember, one quick cut and you're one of us.'

'Not yet,' I said, and he smiled.

'Not yet is good, you're getting closer. But seriously, if you need anything, call me. You have my number.'

I didn't call, but knowing I could made me feel lighter.

~

There's a great Anglican minister I know who likes to crush my hand with a handshake every time. He speaks so passionately at every committal that I feel that doorway to faith almost budging. If a man I feel to be as intelligent, funny, charming and worldly as this believes, then there must be something to it all, yes? If the rabbi I count as a friend, if the Catholic priest I've seen calm and delight crowds with a smile and a splash of holy water, if they believed so assiduously, then there must be something to this God business? Surely?

Perhaps I have seen signs of his presence from time to time.

At one service, the family had had doubts about the final piece of music. They all loved it, and it reminded them of Dad, but they didn't know if they should play it. We had the piece ready, the Bluetooth speaker was primed and ready to go, and as the coffin began to leave the church we hit play ... and the speaker died. No sound whatsoever beyond the squeak of our shoes.

'Told you Dad wouldn't want it in church,' said one of the family. 'We'll play it at the wake.'

At a service for a baby, there was only immediate family in the room sharing stories – grandparents and parents, and us at the desk, keying up video clips or images depending on what we could hear them speaking about. As they talked about the baby's stumble-walk, we ran the 'walking' video; as they talked about the beauty of sleep, we showed images of the child asleep. Then the mother told everyone how she had been shopping for a gift for Dad and had seen a beautiful old wristwatch in an antique store. She'd taken it to a clockmaker for repair, and he'd said he couldn't get it going. She'd tried another specialist, and the same was said again. She held the watch up in the room. 'And this morning it started to tick, as we were leaving to come here. It's ticking now.'

Even I'm not immune to seeing signs. When I got that tattoo after Chris died, I left the parlour with my arm plastic-wrapped and climbed on the bus home. I hit shuffle on my phone, and out of the hundreds of songs that could have played, it was 'Starman' by Bowie. Bowie had been Chris's favourite artist. Coincidence – of course it was – but, man, did it make me feel better.

A ticking watch, a song unplayed, Bowie bursting from head-phones, all little things that suggest that maybe, perhaps, possibly there is something more – that our loved ones aren't gone for good. They are only gone for now.

I'm still an atheist, but 'Starman' makes me feel better about life.

~

On a bad day at work once, one of those days where nothing you say comes out right and nothing you do is effective, I ended up losing my patience. It was a day of being out of the groove, a day where I just couldn't get things right and, impatient with myself, angry with myself, I walked out.

I had my phone and knew work could find me, but I needed to be out of there, to be under the blue sky and clear my head. I walked, I clenched my fists and berated myself for every flaw I could perceive in my abilities, and after a half-hour of stamping my way along streets, I found myself outside a local church that I knew well. It was hot out and I had a sheen of sweat on my forehead. Looking inside, I could see the church was empty, cool and open.

I stepped inside and sat quietly at the back. I let myself cool off and let my thoughts settle. I didn't pray, there was no Biblical epiphany, but there was a calm. I could sit, silently, with my own troubles, and be still. I felt the tide of my thoughts ebb and the clouds I had conjured around myself blow away, and, after an hour or so of silence, I stood up and was surprised to see other people, dotted around the church, silently working their way through their own thoughts.

Outside, I felt better. Walking back to work, I knew I was capable once more. Returning to the office, I found no one had noticed I had walked out. I sat, I refreshed my screen, and when the phone rang, I answered it and found that my words, my actions and my abilities were back in place.

Even for a stalwart, dyed-in-the-wool atheist like me, the church is always open.

Odette

Odette was the last client through our doors before the funeral home moved from its historical location in Bondi. After 130 years, it was time to move, and we were struggling with how deep our roots really sank as we packed, day after day. We were cardboard boxes and chaos, and trying to mask it with shirts and ties. I was on call and taking the arrangements while everyone else was packing.

Just before this had begun there had been an announcement at work that we would shortly have a television crew follow us. Long and slow talks had been happening behind closed doors about an SBS team coming in and, after nervous head-scratching, there'd been a sign-off on the idea. We were told about it as a team, and reactions were uneasy and markedly unenthusiastic. What we do is so personal, so quiet, so dignified, the idea of having a camera crew watching people grieve seemed voyeuristic. It was gradual, though. No one would be in it who didn't want to be, and I didn't want to be. I hung back, stayed outside the camera view, and tried to avoid all conversation with the crew.

They'd pop in and out for certain funerals, and I managed to stay off their radar. They had a request in for any funeral that was out of the ordinary and that could potentially be filmed. Any family that felt unique who, if we could arrange it, would be comfortable on film. Every funeral is out of the ordinary for those attending it, and every family is unique, but the documentary crew meant something beyond the usual of the unusual that we did. Anything colourful or rare. I was determined none of my families would be part of this. It felt wrong. I couldn't imagine anyone wanting their grief recorded.

~

The first call for Odette had been taken by the previous weekend's on-call team member. *Terminally ill, 6–8 months to live. Wants to plan her own funeral.* We didn't know much else. The call sheet was read out amongst us early on a Monday morning, and I put my hand up for it. The call sheet was explicit: the client does not want to have to explain again that she is dying, she wants to plan the funeral.

Working with the terminally ill can be exhausting, as everything we normally don't see is now right in front of us. In all the steps of funeral arranging, the one thing we never really know is the deceased. We come to know their partners, their children and grandchildren, but the deceased themselves to us are photos and stories. Celebrants often say of the dead, 'Now, I never had the pleasure of knowing her.' If the dead were alive, then we wouldn't have heard of them at all.

Pre-paid funerals are often an amusement for the people making them. We'll sit with couples who are getting their lives in order before they move into a care village or nursing home. They laugh at each other's requests.

'I didn't think you'd want a priest,' a wife said once of her husband's statement.

'Well, you know, just in case,' he said.

She laughed at him. 'Just cremate me and give the kids my ashes,' she said.

He blanched. 'That seems so, well, cold.'

She barked a laugh and said, 'Surely it is anything but.'

For the husband, we built up a plan for a funeral mass at a Catholic church he hadn't been to in over thirty years, followed by burial. For the wife, a cremation, no service, ashes to go into the same grave as the husband. They both thought the other's plan was crazy, but two weeks later when I came back with the contracts, they both signed up. The wife added in a small bunch of red roses for her coffin; her husband had insisted that he buy her flowers one more time. The husband had taken the communion out of the funeral service plan, acknowledging, 'I guess I'm not really that Catholic.'

I stood outside as the funeral home behind me was steadily dismantled and watched the road for a terminally ill lady in her forties. I saw a woman walk up, coughing and scowling, and thought, *Okay, here we go.* But beyond scowling at me and coughing in public in the way we did pre-Covid, this woman wasn't for us and she kept walking.

Across the street, I saw several builders snap their heads around, and I followed their gaze to see a beautiful woman in a very short skirt and knee-high boots. She smiled at the attention and looked like life had dealt her a pretty good set of cards. She seemed to be wearing every colour in the crayon box, be it in fabric, jewellery or hair. She crossed the road and walked towards my side of the street, then she turned towards me and kept on coming.

'Richard?' she asked.

I guessed this had to be a friend of my soon-to-be client. The person who had come along to offer support. I racked my brain for the name as I held out my hand.

'Liz?' I asked.

She smiled. 'No. I'm Odette.' Her hand was cool, her nails immaculate, her smile tired but bright. 'Nice to meet you,' she said to me.

'Of course it isn't,' I said back. 'I'm a funeral director.'

She nodded. 'Good point. It's shit to meet you, Richard.'

'Terrible to meet you as well, Odette,' I said, and she smiled again as, behind us, her friend Liz walked up.

'Shall we?' I asked and showed them through the door. 'Please excuse the state of us, we are in the process of moving from here to Waverley. After 130 years it seems we have a lot of history to box up.'

Odette glanced into our swiftly disassembling chapel and at the boxes that were stacked any and every where we could place them.

'How soon until you leave?' she asked. By then it was less than a week. 'Lots of work to do, then,' she said. 'But you'll be able to focus on me?'

I assured her that of course I would. We sat in the arrangement room that was a few weeks away from demolition, and we started.

Or I thought we would. Before I could even write a word, Odette asked me to put my pen down.

'Okay.'

She unfolded a piece of paper, and I saw Liz smile and shake her head slightly.

'I have some very specific requests,' Odette said.

'Good, the more specific you can be, the easier it is for us to know we are doing the right thing.'

'Good answer,' she said and smoothed out the paper. 'Ready?'

'Absolutely.'

She wanted a gloss white coffin; white flowers; her designer shoes to be at the head of the coffin; her dog, Indy, to attend and sit beside the coffin; up to three hundred people to attend at a church that seated only seventy; a violinist; a horse-drawn carriage; white horses; and doves to be released on the day. Oh, and she was friendly with a large contingent of the LGBTQI community, and many of her friends were cross-dressers, and she wanted them to attend as they felt comfortable, in full drag. She wanted colour, as much of it as possible.

My pen was still in my hand, with not a word written.

'What will you be wearing on the day?' she asked me.

'I guess I'll be the only one in black,' I said.

'Will you be wearing that tie?' She pointed at our company tie.

'This is our corporate tie, yes.'

She tutted. 'That's the ugliest fucking tie I have ever seen.'

Liz burst out laughing, I followed along, and Odette waited.

'Then I guess I won't be wearing this tie, then.'

'Do you know *Fifty Shades of Grey*?' she asked me. I confessed that I didn't.

'There is a tie in the film that I love. Can you wear that?'

All I knew of *Fifty Shades of Grey* was the bondage and sex that had people devouring it on the bus and an American library reporting traces of venereal disease being found on the pages of the book – though I'm sure that was an urban myth.

'If we can find it, and purchase some, then I am sure we can.'

'And everything else?' she asked, looking at me with a genuine hope.

'Well,' I opened my file, 'let's go through it all again.'

And we did. And I wrote and wrote and wrote.

Two hours later, she left, and I said we would speak again soon. She'd given me a firm assurance that she would be deceased by Christmas and wanted everything in place by then and had asked if we could speak every week or so to see how things were going. 'I'll do my part,' she said. 'Will you do yours?'

In comparison to what she needed to do for the funeral to happen, my part seemed small.

~

My colleagues were in the kitchenette with a few open bottles of wine. My boss asked how the arrangement meeting had gone, and I summed it up. Horses, carriage, drag queens, violinist, doves.

'The documentary crew would love that,' she said.

I frowned. 'God, no.'

'Well, think about it.'

I had to go; I had an after-hours meeting with another family. Their wife and mother had died from the same cancer that was slowly but inexorably killing Odette. They were at the other end of the scale: they wanted quiet, soft, just immediate family in a chapel, a chance for the children to lay flowers and drawings on Mum's coffin. It's what their mother wanted, they told me, what my wife wanted, the husband told me. We all knew the truth was that the last thing Mum wanted to be was gone, but given we couldn't change that, we could achieve this moment of peace for them before the long years of loss began.

~

The next day at work, the documentary director, Dan, stopped by my desk. 'You had an interesting client yesterday?'

I liked Dan. He had a good mix of enthusiasm and fascination with what we were doing, but I didn't trust him at this point and resented the presence of cameras considerably. I gave him the beats of the funeral plan and the timing.

'Christmas?'

That was the end of the six-month timeframe Odette had given me.

'So, you'll be working with her for the next six months?'

I said I would.

'How is she?'

I said she was bright, colourful, funny, confident.

'And drag queens? The church will allow that?'

I had a lot of discussions to work my way through, but I was certain that they would.

'Would she let us speak with her, do you think?'

Would she? The answer was obvious. If anyone was born for a spotlight, it was Odette. Honestly, though, did I want to be dogged by a camera crew?

'I'll ...'

'We'll treat her well,' Dan said. 'And you'll be in control.'

'I ...'

He smiled at me. 'Go on, just ask her.'

He could be extremely convincing when he wanted to be. It wasn't about me, was it? Of course she would want a camera crew. I knew it before I even asked her the question. Of course she would.

~

I emailed her, summarising our meeting and mentioned at the end that a documentary crew was following us for a few months. I explained that they would like to follow her story, our time together and the eventual funeral. Would she mind a camera crew following along for broadcast on television one day?

Within an hour she came back to me, a big YES to the documentary.

~

For the filming, we had to restage the first meeting. Dan had explained to me how this was Odette's story and the people watching would have to meet Odette as I had met her. It would be hard to bring viewers up to speed unless they saw us meeting. Despite my reservations, I could see what he meant, and I explained this to Odette. I was very conscious of the fact that she had made mention on her first call that she did not want to discuss her illness over and again.

'The camera crew effectively need to see the first time we meet, so if it is okay with you, we'll work through the question set again and you can tell me about ...'

'Your fucking awful ties?'

'Well, yes. I guess so.'

She sounded bright on the phone, and we arranged a time and day, this time to meet at her house rather than my office. The office was now stripped and fast on its way to being brick dust.

I'd told my wife about the camera crew, and she'd told me it was a terrible idea. Awful. She'd given all the considered points: putting your entire character in the hands of an editor, trusting the media industry, and the simple fact of cameras being invasive in what we did for a living. I couldn't disagree at all. I told her about Odette, and she asked me, 'Do you really think this lady wants a camera crew following her as she dies?' Honestly, I did.

Driving out, with Dan and Gary the cameraman in the car, a microphone clipped to my shirt, Dan started asking questions, kind of 'back story on Richard' questions to fill in the blanks. The camera ran, and everything I said was being recorded. I was very uncomfortable and chose my answers slowly. We found a park in Paddington, which was a small miracle. They hung back to film me walking, which in itself was extremely strange, and I found myself thinking so hard about how to walk that I almost lost my balance.

Odette opened the door, dressed amazingly again, and I introduced her to Dan and Gary. I told her we could stop at any time if this became too much and did my best to talk her out of it. Odette had a friend downstairs where we sat by her back door, and I asked the friend to step in at any point if all of this seemed too ridiculous. I'd have asked the dog to stop this as well if I thought it might step in. No one called halt, though, and Odette and I sat, camera trained on us, microphones clipped to us, and we began (again).

Quietly, and as comfortably as I could manage, we worked through our first meeting again. I asked the questions, Odette gave the answers, she read me her list, drag queens, doves, horse-drawn carriage, white horses, three hundred people at a church that would seat seventy at best, and for the camera I wrote the points down, basically running my pen over the words I had written previously.

Dan had told me, and had spoken to Odette about it as well, that I would have to ask the question as to how long Odette had to live. The question was grotesque, but Odette told me it was okay, so I stopped and put my pen down and asked her: 'If you don't mind, what time frame are we looking at here?'

Odette took a deep breath and said it again, as I imagine she had said to her children and to her friends and to me once before. 'The doctors tell me I will be gone by Christmas.'

Dan looked down at the floor. Gary blinked and quickly wiped his eye.

Then Odette asked me, 'What will you be wearing at my funeral?'

I felt the needle settle back into the groove on the record and said as I had said before, 'Well, it sounds like I will be the only one in black on the day.'

'Will you be wearing that tie?' she asked me again.

'Well, it is our corporate tie, yes.'

Emphatically, scorching and wonderful, she stared at me and stated, 'That is the ugliest fucking tie I have ever seen.'

I laughed and felt things were okay. This was ridiculous, a camera crew following us. She knew it, I knew it, but it was okay. My tie was fucking hideous, and she was enjoying herself, enjoying the attention. As she told me later, 'This whole documentary should be about me. I'll call Dan and try and get him to change it.'

She hugged Dan and the cameraman at the end of the meeting, and I could see they'd both been affected, having sat with someone so utterly aware that death was coming and that her last Christmas had already happened.

Outside, Dan was astonished. Gary was entranced. 'She looks amazing on screen,' he said.

Dan nodded. 'She sounds amazing as well.'

Then he sighed and rubbed his cheeks. 'Jesus, this is going to be hard.'

~

Over the next six months Odette and I met many times, often with the camera team in tow.

One evening, around 7pm, Dan asked me if I could phone Odette at the hospital she was in. 'It's her last birthday. We want to film both sides of a conversation.'

Her last birthday. Most people don't know that they are celebrating their last birthday, but Odette did. And she had convinced the hospital to let her friends in, to let a camera crew in and to let some of her friends come in drag. Honestly, I think she could have convinced Trump to admit he was bald, she was that hypnotic. You wanted to do the things she asked; you wanted her to be your friend.

'What are we supposed to talk about?' I asked Dan, as everything was pretty much on track. A series of arrangements with no fixed date, a series of phone calls with no actual deadline.

'Just talk to her, mate. She wants you to call her and wish her happy birthday.'

Around 6pm a man came and clipped a microphone to me at work. He nestled himself in with a camera, and my boss, who'd hung back to make sure I was travelling okay, settled quietly at her end of the office. Bang on time I called Odette, and when she answered I could hear cheering and laughter in the background.

'Happy birthday, my friend,' I said.

She swiftly reminded me that this was her last birthday. The words stuck, scratched themselves into the walls.

She asked me how her funeral was going, and I gave her an update that she already had. Horse and cart: check. Doves: check. Posh shoes: to come. Flowers: arranged. Coffin: arranged. Church: appeased. Marquee: arranged.

'It sounds beautiful,' she said, and I knew she was wanting to see it, hoping the heaven rumours were true and that she would be able to sit ringside and watch as everybody missed her, talked about her, loved her.

I heard champagne pop and laughter and said that I had better go. I wished her happy birthday again, and she wished me well.

The cameraman unclipped me and said something along the lines of 'This is a fucking strange job you have'.

~

I'd mentioned to Odette that the horse and cart were arranged, and they were. I'd also called the local police and talked them through the plan, told them about the horse and cart moving approximately 200 yards on Old South Head Road. The police officer I had spoken to had listened, made notes and told me that that was all fine and I had nothing to worry about. He said I should just call back and let them know when I had a date for the funeral.

I had nothing to worry about. It was fine, they said.

~

Towards the end of the six months, as Odette's health was becoming more and more affected, we met at St Peter's Anglican Church in Watsons Bay to effectively walk ourselves through the day. We'd met there once before, without the camera, to discuss with the minister if we could erect a marquee and have Odette's drag friends attend. He'd told us he was not averse to it but wanted us to meet a few other people to discuss the presence of cameras. A few weeks later, Dan, my boss and I met in the city with the church bursars and the ministers, and we talked through things again, without Odette. We promised respect, we agreed to film the key parts of the service that the church would want heard and, after a few hours, we had their permission.

I'd arranged with the church to have this hour free for Odette to walk through and see where her coffin would be, and then where her ashes would be. It was a wet weekday. Dan met me at the church ahead of time. As we waited for Odette, he had me stand by a tree as Gary focused the camera on the raindrops on the leaves with me blurred in the background.

'Is that your Terrence Malick shot?' I asked.

Odette arrived, now moving slower, speaking slower. She was in a lot of pain by then, but was masking it, and was still dressed impeccably. She was cold, and the cameraman slipped off his scarf and gave it to her. We walked, we talked, and then we sat together on a pew in the church. I was talking to her about who would be where on the day: Indy the dog would be sitting just there, the flowers placed there, your coffin (hard words to say) will be just up these steps. Odette cracked. She told me she was scared. I hugged her instinctively and told her of course she was, what was happening was a fucking tragedy.

Later I forgot about the swearing. After the show aired, I copped more than a little flak from the funeral industry for swearing in the church. I'm still an atheist but I am very aware of the privilege we have in going into these places and being trusted to deliver funerals there. At the time I said it, though, I wasn't a funeral director, I was Odette's friend. Over those months, all the text messages, the emails and meetings, we had become friends. She knew about my family, my kids, my wife. I knew about her children and the way she spoke of them, with such awe and love and admiration.

It was fucking tragic what was happening.

~

'Are you going away over Christmas?' Dan asked me.

'I'll be away in January, yes.'

'What do we do if Odette dies while you are away?'

'Well, I guess one of my colleagues will conduct on the day.'

Dan looked gravely at me. 'That won't work.'

I realised it wouldn't. If nothing else, I had promised Odette I would be there. I would collect her from the hospital. I would do everything I had said. Life was getting in the way of her death, and I felt conflicted as to what to do.

'Where will you be?' Dan asked me, and I told him.

'Okay,' he said, 'so if she passes away while you are off, we'll get a helicopter to you.'

'Wow,' I said.

When I told Odette, she laughed, and we shared a menthol cigarette on her deck. 'A helicopter?'

I nodded.

'I want to go in a helicopter,' she said, and I pictured a white-horse-drawn helicopter arriving at church.

While we smoked, she looked at the tattoo I'd had done to remember Chris. Large lettering – PROM – on my arm. She asked me about Chris, and I told her about him, about our friendship and about picking him up from hospital.

'When you pick me up, they'll be filming, yes?'

The reality of how strange this all was now really started to hit me. 'Yes,' I replied.

'Then roll your sleeves up, let's get Chris in the scene as well.'

I did. When the day finally came that I had to drive to the hospital, with Gary in tow, I rolled up my sleeve and had Chris there on my arm as I collected Odette from the same mortuary where I had collected him.

And when the documentary aired, I got flak for that as well. Rolled-up shirt sleeves, tattooed arm. 'That's how you guys do transfers, is it?' I was asked, and have been asked several times since.

No, it's not. But it was that day.

~

Almost precisely on time, Odette died.

Liz called me to say she'd passed on a Saturday morning a few weeks before the Christmas she had been told she wouldn't reach. 'Well,' I sighed, 'then I guess we put the best laid plans into action.'

I immediately started with the calls. First to the minister at the church. He advised me straightaway that he couldn't do it, he was tied up, unavailable. It just couldn't be done. I asked if I could bring another minister in, and he said if I thought I could, then I should go for it.

I called the local bishop. He was warm and welcoming and humorous, and such a perfect fit for Odette. Without hesitation, he said, 'Of course.' When I told him about the television cameras and the documentary, he was unfazed.

Next came the transfer (and the tattoo) and the long drive with Odette. Gary was in the passenger seat filming me the whole way, peppering me with questions. At one point, having known Odette now for seven or eight months, I said it was very strange to have Odette with us, but no longer with us.

He turned his camera and said, 'Say that again.'

Television dictated I repeat once more with feeling something I had said accidentally and earnestly already.

Gary was distracted. After a while he admitted he'd had a crush on Odette during the last six months of filming her.

'She was beautiful,' he said.

She absolutely was.

Piece by piece, we put things in order. The marquee was arranged. The horse and cart arranged. The police called and notified of the date, the route and the horses. All was well, and steadily the day of the funeral approached, dictated by the availability of the church and the venue for the wake. This close to Christmas, the wake was hard to lock in, but they did their best for Odette and a room was secured. Just under ten days after her death we were ready for her funeral. Odette's voice was in my ear the whole time, nudging me onwards.

One evening, three days before the service, the local police called me and told me I couldn't have the horse and cart. They told me if the horse caused an issue on Old South Head Road at 10am then buses would be running late in Mosman by 2pm. I explained that I had already called and talked through this and gave the name of the officer. I was told that officer was wrong, and I couldn't have the horse and cart. I'd have to drive the coffin to the gates of the church, load the coffin into the cart and clip-clop twenty metres into the church and then do the same in reverse afterwards.

'I can't do that,' I said. 'It was her wish for the horse and cart.' I explained again that I'd already called the police and asked them what they needed of me and answered all their questions. I explained about the television cameras and how long this had been planned.

The man softened, ever-so-slightly. He told me to email through every detail, and then gave me seven or eight email addresses. I said I would by 8am the next day. He also told me that, on the day, if I was permitted to have the horse and cart, there would be a police car parked opposite the church to ensure my horses didn't step an inch outside of my agreed route, didn't cause mayhem on the streets of Sydney.

All I could say was, 'Thanks.'

I spent the night working on the email, had it read and reviewed the next day and, in between fielding calls from Dan and trying to reassure him that the horses would happen and hearing him contemplate losing his money-shot moment, I sent it on and crossed my fingers and hoped.

~

We were cleared for the horse and cart with forty-eight hours to go. The marquee was going up, Odette's *Fifty Shades of Grey* ties were distributed among the funeral crew, and my boss sat with me the morning before and asked if there was anything I needed.

'Uhm, yeah.'

'What?'

'Can you come along tomorrow. Just in case we ... uhm, I don't know, need to bribe the police on the horse-and-cart issue?'

She looked appalled and more than a little afraid. 'Really?'

'I've no idea, but if something goes wrong, I'd really feel better if you were there.'

She nodded. 'I'm not sure about bribery, but I'll be there.'

~

That morning I was a whirlwind of anxiety and tension. I hadn't had much sleep the night before and, on leaving home, Mel had hugged me and wished me well. We aren't a morning hug kind of couple; she's always busy with something and I'm always away early and the kids are a tumbling battlefield of lost homework and flung-together sandwiches. A five-second hug helped, and then Tilda rushed out and hugged me as well. Sandy, realising that something was obviously happening that he'd forgotten about, joined in the hug.

'Thanks,' I said, and Mel told me it would all be fine.

~

In the final hour and a half before every funeral I am always concerned that I have missed something – that I've forgotten to book the venue or the priest or the flowers. I worry that the hearse will break down, or the coffin will slip from our grip. In fact, right up until the moment when the celebrant or clergy commences the service, I am worried. One minister we work with is notorious for arriving right at the last moment for services at crematorium chapels, and each time my heart starts hammering as I wonder and watch and wait, and then, just as I'm about to fully panic, he appears, wise, warm and calm. I find myself checking work emails, verifying over and over that, yes, I booked the hire cars, the church, the flowers, everything. Self-doubt is relentless. Much as I know I can do this job and do it well, I still expect past me to betray present me with some unfinished aspect of the planning.

That morning, I was even more trepidatious than usual. We left early, earlier than usual, and found the marquee in late-stage construction at St Peter's. There were chairs piled up all around and maybe twelve people on site, busily building. The hearse was going to arrive down the hill at the driveway of the neighbouring Catholic church, where Odette's coffin would be transferred into the horse and cart. When I'd asked the Catholic church if we could use their driveway for the horse and cart, they had said, 'Of course, anything for our neighbours.'

I knew the horse and cart would drive past the front of St Peter's on the way to collect Odette, so I had a team member watching as we started placing the chairs.

Australia did its blue-sky thing, and sweat prickled my forehead. The *Fifty Shades of Grey* tie was cinched tight and, I must admit, looked rather dashing. I felt very *Casablanca* and wished we had hats as part of our uniform.

A lady with a box of doves arrived. My friend Michelle Bova, the AV specialist, was on site connecting cables to the large screen in the marquee that would show the events from inside the church. The documentary caught Michelle giving me a hug, but it didn't catch me saying, 'I'm terrified,' and her replying, 'You got this.' The bishop, seeing me hug Michelle, came over and had a hug himself and also told me, 'It will all be fine, Richard.'

My colleague Lee called out to me, 'Hey, boss,' and nodded to the passing truck with the horse and the cart on it going by behind me. I sent Lee and Peter off down the hill to liaise with the horses while I stayed behind, setting out the chairs. Michelle got my attention and then nodded to the entry to the church: a police car had pulled up with two officers looking across at us.

'Oh well,' I sighed and walked towards them.

I introduced myself and asked how they were. They told me they were well, and I ran them through the schedule: the horse and cart would come up the hill and into the church grounds, and then, an hour later, the horse and cart would leave the church and return down the hill to Our Lady Star of the Sea. The two officers nodded, and then one smiled.

'Sounds like a good plan,' he said.

'I hope so. I guess you're here in case things go wrong?'

He smiled again. 'She'll be right, mate.'

'Thanks for being here, if you need a bottle of water or anything just give us a wave,' I said, and they wished me well. Walking back, I panicked. I'd only meant a bottle of water. Had it sounded like I was offering them a bribe?

'It's a beautiful day for it,' the lady with the doves said as I walked by. It really was. An old colleague used to say, 'Sydney has her legs out today.' She really did. The sky was blue, the temperature perfect, the sun painting us beautifully.

I felt the tension ease and returned to the church as people started to arrive. Cars pulled in and people gathered, signing the book and taking the orders of service. Then the drag queens appeared, beautiful birds of paradise walking into view. Big smiles and warm hearts and exactly what Odette had wanted, exactly as she had told me so many times. Music was playing and jigsaw pieces were falling into place and the clock was ticking.

Dan came up behind me and asked how things were going.

'Well, I hope,' I said.

Like everyone else, he told me I had this. It would go great. Then he said, 'This is heartbreaking, I'm honestly close to tears.' His eyes were damp.

I knew exactly how he felt. It was heartbreaking. But I was so wired on adrenaline that I couldn't stop to think about it.

'I know, mate. I'll talk to you about it later,' I said as, right on cue, the horse and cart clipped into view. Everyone turned to see Odette arriving in a white-horse-drawn hearse with a top-hatted driver. Lee was sitting up beside the driver and trying desperately not to smile as the horses led the way.

'You came on the horse and cart?' I asked him.

'Stay with the coffin, boss, that's my job.' His smile was barely withheld. 'And that was fun!'

Sydney had her legs out, and Lee looked fantastic.

~

The bishop started the funeral with the words 'Death sucks', and I heard the crowd exhale almost as one, knowing that they were in good hands – safe hands. The service passed in a blur. Indy the dog sat obediently by the coffin. The eulogies spoke of the sparkle and humour Odette had, right until the end. The shoes were on her coffin. The flowers were in place. Everything was as she had described to me at that first meeting when the builders had turned their heads and wolf-whistled the woman in the short skirt and the knee-high boots.

We carried her to the hearse after the service, and her children gathered together, held up a dove each and released them. Above us, a drone captured everything. I wanted to bat it away at that point, this being such a raw moment of grief, but later when I saw the footage, I had to admit it was beautiful.

The bishop and I stood in front of the horses to walk them away but very swiftly moved to one side. A hearse will proceed slowly, at walking pace, whereas horses choose their own pace. The policemen were out of their car stopping traffic for us, and the horses and Odette left with ease. The policemen nodded to me and said, 'Nice job.'

My boss was by the church gate looking nervously at the police car. 'I think we are okay,' I said.

A few minutes later our black hearse drove by silently, and Odette was away to the crematorium. Her guests were making their way down the hill to the Watsons Bay Boutique Hotel. Michelle was already there, photographing the wake, and she gave me another hug and promised to see me later for a beer.

Odette's father appeared in front of me and shook my hand and asked me to please stay for a drink. He thanked me for what we had done for Odette as the room thronged with champagne, canapes and good memories of a good woman. I didn't stay for the beer. Now Odette was safely away I felt it was time for the black suits and the *Fifty Shades of Grey* ties to also disappear.

We melted into the background and returned home. That night, at Chris's favourite bar, Jangling Jacks in Potts Point, Dan the documentary man, Gary the cameraman, my boss and Michelle, my AV friend, sat at the corner by Chris's seat. Chris's partner Charlie came through the door and gave me a hug and we drank, toasting Odette, toasting Chris, toasting love and loss and memory.

My word, did I drink.

~

On the night the documentary aired, we held a special screening at the Randwick Ritz cinema. Dan stood up and introduced things, thanking our funeral home and his crew and other folk, and then thanking Odette. The brave and beautiful Odette, who'd allowed the cameras to follow her over her last six months and who had left her mark on everyone who had met her. I was sat in the crowd with my daughter. As Odette's funeral played out on the big screen, Tilda saw her from our first meeting through to her funeral. Afterwards she said, 'She seemed lovely, Dad.'

Seeing it all in one rush, I couldn't answer. I thought of Dan telling me his heart was breaking on the day of the funeral and finally allowed mine to do the same.

A Little Death

I've never really thought I could die. Near-miss car accidents, just-caught bannisters when tripping on the stairs, cars screeching to a halt when I was a kid crossing the road dangerously on my bike: I always seemed to step around it, managing to avoid injury or worse. Like most people who don't find themselves in hospital or trapped in a crashed car, I seemed to live away from the moments that fill television dramas.

When I collapsed in a church and found myself sprawled under the stained-glass window, head spinning, heart hammering, alone and afraid, the thought started to form. In hospital shortly after, I started thinking about it a lot.

~

My body hadn't been behaving as it should. I was being pulled to the left every time I walked. A bad headache had been dogging me for a few days, and my vision was odd. Mel, whenever I say I have a headache, tells me to drink more water, and I had convinced myself I must be dehydrated. I was gulping down a bottle of water as often as I could and impatiently waiting for this head pain to dissipate. I have a habit of drinking cheap red wine – which I know isn't healthy, and I know has likely turned my insides into wet red sand – and I wondered if I had finally gone too cheap with my choice. Had I drunk antifreeze, or had a bottle been off and my palette too degraded to notice?

I was driving the hearse on this day, so had spent the morning washing and wiping down the vehicle, blacking the tyres and replenishing the tissues and the memorial book pages on the clipboards. My hearse looked good, and I had awkwardly loaded the coffin and flowers with some help. I had half an hour before departure and was knocking back another bottle of water as my vision swam and my left leg seemed determined to do its own thing.

I then had a moment of horror. Without being aware it was happening, I had lost control of my bowel. Not hugely, but enough. I moved to the bathroom and saw myself in the mirror, pale and beaded with sweat. I really wasn't well, but I had a funeral to do, and I couldn't step back. The problem with this kind of work is that we always think we are the only ones who can do it – that we are the essential cog to the machine. We must be there; we must fulfil our role. This isn't ego, it's simply not wanting to let someone down. We are a small team, and if one of us drops out it's hard to reconfigure.

I cleaned myself as best I could and went to the mortuary for a can of deodorant. I threw away my underwear and grabbed a pair of cycle shorts from my locker. I was bumping into the walls. My head was pounding. I just had to do this funeral and then I'd be okay.

My colleague came down saying it was time to go and I saw my left hand was a blur. My left leg not obeying.

'Can you drive?' I asked.

'You okay?'

'Yeah, sure. Just feeling a bit dizzy.'

He drove, I rode shotgun. Two colleagues were following us in another car and, once there, we carried the coffin in. Walking with the coffin was actually easier, as I had the weight on my right pulling me into line. My colleague could see I was off and stood me at the lectern to take signatures as people arrived. I held on to the stand, my vision swooping, and fixed my face.

'Welcome, please add your name ... Welcome, please add your name.'

Today was different. Today, all the names were familiar. Australian television celebrities. Big, swooping signatures. The more famous you are, the larger the signature, I have found. I handed the pen over and struggled to take it back, I felt myself listing to the left and forced myself upright. I watched familiar faces blur as they moved to my left.

My colleague was watching me. 'You're not right, Richard,' he said.

I finally admitted it out loud: 'I'm really not.'

'Sit at the back of the church,' he said.

A musician sang at the end of the service, solo with a guitar. It would have been a great thing to see but I was clutching the seat, feeling the world whoosh around and around, trying to hold my stomach in check.

I stood to carry out, my left leg trying to flail, and again relied on the weight to my right to pull me into line. I made it to the hearse and my colleague asked me to go back into the church to get the trolley. I stepped cautiously, took the side door into the now empty church, and collapsed.

~

I was still half-convinced that I was just dehydrated, so I bought a bottle of lurid blue rehydration drink. I caught a cab home as soon as we were back, texting Mel that I was going home sick. I gulped down the Gatorade in the cab, finishing it as I was walking into my home. I lay down on the sofa and tried to believe in the science: *I'll get better now; the drink says rehydrate.* I put one hand on the floor to stop myself from falling off the planet.

Mel appeared in the doorway.

'You okay?' she asked. To me she was swooping in and out of sight. She was there and then whisked away.

'I think something is wrong,' I said, and as the words left my mouth, the blue drink surged upwards. I rushed by her, bouncing off the walls and fell into the bathroom as the drink came back up.

'Jesus Christ, what's wrong?' Mel asked.

'I'm not well.' I fell to the left. She helped me up again and kept me upright.

'You need the hospital,' Mel said, and I remember the relief of being led, of someone else taking control of a situation I had lost all grasp on.

~

At triage, a nurse came to see me. She was Irish, friendly and reassuring. She asked what was wrong and by now I was barely able to look at anyone, keeping my eyes down or closed. I told her about the dizziness and the sickness.

'Anything else now?' she asked. I admitted to losing control of my bowel.

'Oh, pet, this hasn't been a good day for you now, has it?'

Here is our daughter, Matilda, adorably oblivious to the fact that she's heading to hospital for emergency, life-saving surgery. It was this experience, and a careless comment from a colleague, that set me on a career change to becoming a funeral director.

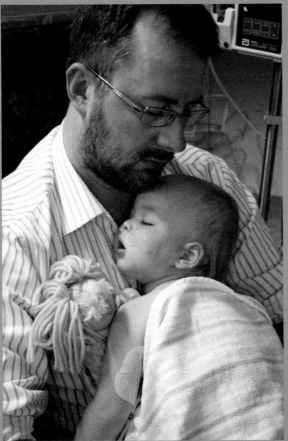

When Matilda finally woke up, she crawled towards me and said, 'Daddy, away,' and then fell asleep on my lap. She had come through, and she was here in my arms.

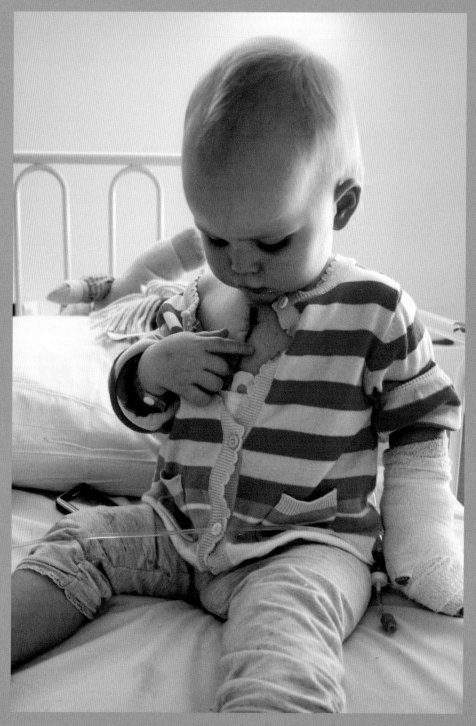

Here is Matilda exploring her new scar in the recovery ward. The bandage on her left hand had a splint inside it to keep the skin grafts on her palm stretched as much as possible.

Matilda had her last surgery in December 2022, marking the end of thirteen years of procedures and pain. She has been incredibly brave throughout, and the PTSD I still carry from this experience guides me in my job every day.

Three beautiful humans – Sandy, Melinda and Matilda – and myself, moving into my lighthouse keeper phase. (Photograph by Emma Fyfe.)

When I was taken on at entry level by a funeral home at age 40, I was advised they didn't really like beards. For the first time in years, I shaved, and I discovered that beneath the beard lay a bullfrog. (Image credit: Funeral Video Australia)

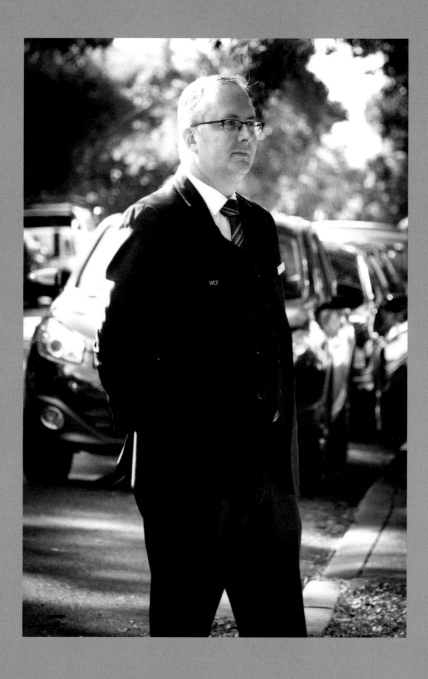

A selfie taken at a mortuary training course. Theoretically, I can perform the basics of preparation for a deceased person: closing the eyes and mouth, washing and dressing, removing a pacemaker. I am happy for this to remain theoretical.

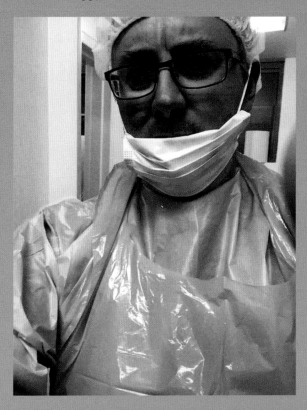

Chris Murray, my friend, by far the coolest person I have ever known, at his spiritual home, Jangling Jacks. (Image credit: Erin Reeves)

This is Odette, an amazing woman who engaged me when she had six months to live to help prepare her unique funeral. We worked together constantly over menthol cigarettes and tea – she'd text me at all hours with wild ideas about her ashes and I'd calm her down with bad jokes. Above is a still from the documentary *The Secret Life of Us* by Mint Pictures, and below was the last time I saw her alive – one last menthol and a hug.

Odette planned her funeral down to every last detail, including her designer shoes to be at the head of her gloss-white coffin and her dog to attend and sit beside it, a violinist, doves to be released on the day, a horse-drawn carriage (pictured above) and her own hand-picked ties to be worn by us (pictured below). At the end of that unforgettable day, at a bar with my colleagues, I toasted Odette and one of the most heartbreaking and wonderful ceremonies we had ever been involved in. (Images credit: Funeral Video Australia)

My son, Sandy, looks delighted to be doing two weeks' work experience with his old man in a funeral home. Here he is proudly displaying his first ever Windsor knot.

In over ten years of funeral work, I have aged at least twenty. I likely look exactly how I pictured a funeral director would all those years ago when someone asked what I would do if Matilda died during surgery. To have a job that I love is a privilege.

She lifted my chin and looked at my eyes.

'I'm just going to do a quick test. Try and look at me.'

She gently shook my chin and stared at me. Then her face fell to serious, and she said, 'I'll be back in just one minute.'

She came back with a doctor, who sat in front of me and held my chin. She performed the same shake and her face became concerned.

'We're going to admit you,' she said.

Mel, standing by the door, said, 'Is everything okay?'

The doctor, as calmly as possible, said, 'Richard is showing signs of either an inner ear infection or a stroke. Is there any history of stroke in the family?'

'No,' I said.

'Didn't your grandmother die of a stroke?'

I tried to think through, but it was getting harder. I felt like now I was in hospital I could crawl into the darkness inside and swim back up later when whatever was wrong had been fixed for me.

'Yes. Yes, she did. I think.' My mouth felt fuzzy.

'How old was she?' the doctor asked.

I tried to think. I fought to think.

'She was in her forties,' Mel said for me. I was in my forties. They took me to a bed and told me not to worry, while Mel stood there worrying. I clung to the bed frame so as not to fall off.

Everything was pulling me to the floor, and I was so very tired.

This was when I wondered if this was the slow trickle of pebbles that would become a landslide. Was this the beginning of my end? My nan had had several strokes in quick succession – was this the first of my own?

I remember trying to wrestle with those thoughts, but they kept slipping away. I was so tired and just wanted to close my eyes. And I did. If this was death, I was tired enough to let it slip me away.

~

They put me into the stroke ward. I was taken for an MRI.

Before I could go in, I called to the nurse apologetically, 'Excuse me, I'm sorry, but I think I am going to throw up.'

'Oh, gosh,' the nurse replied and moved quickly to get a sick bag. 'Just hold on, my love,' she said, and I held on, my throat quickly filling.

She handed me the bag and I retched. This was far from a black suit and calm dignity. I was in a hospital gown and looking sallow. After one of the doctors had said he was becoming more convinced that this was an inner ear infection, Mel had gone home to pick up the kids from school and explain to them where Dad was. All I could think was that I was in the belly of one of the hospitals from which I regularly collected the deceased. I was a few floors up from the mortuary. Not far from Medical Records. Not far from the cashier. My own paperwork was right now being developed.

'I'm sorry,' I said as the nurse took the bag from me.

'Oh, hush,' she said. 'Stop being so polite.'

~

I was put in a bed opposite an elderly lady who was struggling with the fact of a mixed-gender ward. Beside her was an elderly man. Opposite, another elderly man. I was the youngest there by far. In the rare moments where my vision settled, I could see mops of white hair and pigeon chests. I pulled my glasses off and tried to stay still.

Mel and the kids came to see me. Sandy and Tilda were wide-eyed and afraid. I tried to reassure them with whatever lopsided jokes I could. They slept in bed with their mum that night. I slept in the hospital in fits and starts. Each time I rolled onto my side I felt the tube in my arm yank at my skin.

I woke up at one point to hear a man to my right shouting, 'Nurse, nurse, shitting!' With my glasses off I could see a blue blurred nurse rushing to a white bed, and then a sudden fountain of brown.

The elderly lady opposite me gasped. The man was whisked away, cleaned and returned as I drifted into confusion again. The nurses came and checked on us one by one, calm, friendly and warm.

~

In the morning a doctor came to see me. He finally confirmed that this was an inner ear infection and definitely not a stroke. He then told me about the chin shaking test they'd done yesterday. It had been invented in Australia, he told me. They shake the chin and watch the eyes. For strokes (and inner ear infections) the eyes roll independently of each other. He told me my eyes were wonderful for showing this and asked if I would mind if student doctors came to see me during the day.

'That's fine,' I said, figuring that if something useful came of this, then that was a good thing. As I tell the kids, if you can help, then do help – in any circumstance. All I had to do to help was lie there being ill. That seemed easy enough.

A few minutes later, two young men came in. They interviewed me on my symptoms and history and then each took a turn shaking my head and watching my eyes. They nodded and tried to hide their grins.

'Does it look odd?' I asked.

Trying to keep professional faces, one of them replied. 'Well, your left eye is rolling on its own while your right stays focused on me.'

From my side, it was like looking at a someone while a ghost tried to leave their body.

They left. And then more came. And then more.

Trainee after trainee came in, in pairs, in threes, clusters of six or seven. They sat before me, asked me questions, asked for the history of my situation, and then they shook my chin and tried to keep a straight face as my left eye rolled around untethered and my right stayed focused on them.

'It's okay,' I said to one group of three. 'I don't mind if you laugh.'

'That's wild,' one young guy said, and I nodded as his ghost tried to tear free of his face.

~

A little while later my friend Peter Burns came in. A different chap to the Peter I work with. Peter Burns worked in the hospital and had heard from Mel that I was there.

He sat and tried not to laugh as I told him about the old man and the fountain of shit from the night before. Then he told me, 'There's a huge group of trainees out by the elevators all talking about some mad fella with crazy eyes.'

'That would be me,' I said. Two more aspirational doctors came in, and Peter watched them sit, take their notes and then shake my chin.

'Jesus, do that again,' he said, looking over their shoulders. My left eye did its thing, rolling like tumbleweed and stretching the spirits from their skin as half my vision spun.

'That's fucking insane,' one of the trainees said, forgetting himself. He rushed to apologise, but I said it was okay. 'You should see it from my side.'

As Peter left, he glanced down the corridor. 'There's lots of them,' he said, and grinned at me. 'I mean, like, a lot.'

It was okay. They were all good-natured folk, and I was the weird man with the wobbly eye.

'Behave, now,' he said to the trainees as he left. 'He's a very old man, and he's in a very bad way.'

Two more heads appeared around the curtain. Looking nervous now.

'Excuse me, sir, but we've been asked to—'

'Come in and shake my head?'

'Yes.'

I heard Peter laughing as he left.

Another hand settled on my chin; another trainee doctor asked me about my medical history.

'Sh— wow,' the trainee said. 'How does that look for you?'

Three ... two ... one ... release the ghost from the face.

~

Medical staff amaze me. I've only once met a nurse who didn't seem unflappably calm. I was at the hospital to collect a baby. I usually come in from the back of the hospital, wearing trousers and a shirt (no jacket), and try to be as discreet as possible. I was riding the elevator from the basement when this nurse stepped in. She looked exhausted.

'Are you okay?' I asked, and she pulled a 'Yeah, fine' from somewhere.

'Okay,' I said. Then added, 'But I don't think you are.'

'No. It's the end of a long shift,' she said, and it was clear that whatever had happened during that shift had been wrenching, and I wished her safe home.

She exited the lift. As much as I see behind the curtain, into the corners where most people don't look, it's less than all that is seen by nurses, doctors and ambulance staff. They rush to those corners, and try to pull people back into the safety of the light. My hands reach people when they are cool; hospital staff have their hands on people when they are still vital, still hopeful. People tell me they can't imagine doing what I do but, really, I don't think it is that confronting. (Perhaps sometimes I get it, at dinnertime when my daughter tells me about her day and show rehearsals, and Mel tells us about one of her students, and Sandy grunts and says his day was okay, and I say, 'I was speaking to a woman on the phone today. She was pre-planning her partner's funeral, and she suddenly stopped talking, and then told me her partner had just died, right then and there.')

It's mostly after the fact for me. For us. We arrive after hope has ended. For the nurse, hope is there every day, and I can only imagine that watching hope leave can be exhausting.

In hospitals we are handed paperwork from someone whose job it is to process the files of the deceased. This was my Nan's job many years ago. It was my father's mother who handed the bag of clothing over after my mother lost her mum to a stroke.

In hospitals we used to go to the cashier with a cheque for the cremation documents before the process was updated. Another staff member checked our paperwork and clipped a receipt to our Transfer Authority, then another added the document for the deceased. An ordered, dignified process of checking and double-checking at every step before a person was released to me from the mortuary.

Most mortuaries have a large walk-on scale where the trolley is wheeled for the body to be weighed. When we go to them, I stand on the scale and have watched the needle inch upwards year by year, mentally disassociating myself from the bodies just behind the doors in their body bags.

The final staff member we see is the mortuary attendant, who smiles at us, makes small talk and is warm and friendly. They open the bag for us to check for valuables and to check the wristband of the body. The body will be from surgery, or the cardio ward, or intensive care, or the stroke ward. The skin will be cold to the touch, lips parted, eyes open. A hospital gown protecting their dignity. Sometimes I glimpse tattoos. Sometimes gold teeth are reflecting the light dully from inside their mouth.

We check, check again, and slide the body onto our trolley. We sign the body out, the final piece of paperwork, and then we leave.

~

Before I left the hospital after my inner ear adventure, Mel and I went for a coffee, and I tried to feel normal. I made myself look at the books on the shelves and the patients and families around me. I tried to be a typical hospital patient, sick but improving.

Instead, I was the guy in the cafe noticing funeral teams discreetly slip through the doors with clipboards, chasing their paperwork. I was noticing the white vans sneaking round to the mortuary to collect the deceased.

Now that I wasn't dying, I was keen to get back to work.

~

A short while ago I was speaking on the phone to Aurelia, a colleague at one of the crematoriums. She sounded tired.

'You okay?' I asked. She told me in a rush that this was her first day back. That her husband had had a heart attack a week or so earlier.

'We were on a bush walk and ... he just dropped.'

'Shit.'

'We were just starting the walk. By the car park. If we'd been further on, then ... well.'

She'd pulled him to the car and driven him straight to the hospital, where he'd been operated on almost immediately, waking up to find he had two stents in his body.

'Wow,' I said. 'That's crazy. I mean, for him. He's woken up better, not even knowing he was ill.'

'That's such a man thing to say,' she told me.

I agreed. 'Mate, I'm terrified of diagnosis. Life is easier if you don't know about the timebomb building up in you. Imagine the stress if he'd known that he could have a heart attack any moment. If you were waiting on surgery with a date a year hence but knowing that, any day now, he might fall?'

'When is the last time you went to the doctor?' she asked me, and I confessed that it would have to have been ten years ago, or more.

There was a silence on the line, and then she said, 'Go to the doctor.'

She's a good friend and when a friend tells you something, there is more of an obligation to listen. I really didn't want to see a doctor, but I did. I did the check-up: kicked the tyres, checked under the hood.

I had my blood taken. That's the bit I don't like; it's like letting all your secrets slip out without even knowing what your own secrets are. Yes, I can hide the fact that I think 'Moonlight Shadow' by Mike Oldfield is a classic song and that I have residual fantasies of being a store mannequin with Kim Cattrall, but whatever is in my blood is a secret of mine that I have no idea about.

A week later I went back, and the doctor told me, with considerable cheer, that I was now diabetic. It's in my family on my mother's side. 'And now it's your turn,' he told me. Cut out sugars. Cut out this and that. Learn the new world order. No rice or pasta. Lots of leafy greens. I mean *lots* of leafy greens. I have more appointments ahead in order to learn more about this condition, and I guess whatever is written by my future death doctor may yet tie in with the diabetes.

I called Aurelia back a few days later.

'I went to the doctor,' I said.

She told me this was a good thing.

'No. I'm diabetic now, and I'm entirely blaming you.'

She told me she didn't care if I blamed her: I knew I was diabetic now, and could do something about it. 'After all, you were diabetic before you went to the doctor, you just didn't know.'

'Hmph,' I said, and then reluctantly agreed with her. 'Thanks for insisting,' I said, begrudgingly.

Since the time in the hospital, I do think about my death more. I try to chase my extra weight away, with limited success. I eat huge amounts of spinach and rocket, hoping to make up for past KFC transgressions. I drink water, trying to rehydrate the drought of red wines past. Like most middle-aged people, I am becoming more aware that death is coming, though hopefully now delayed by my new diabetic knowledge. Death is waiting at the side of the road, enjoying the Snickers bar that I am not allowed to eat anymore.

I was driving while on call one night, and I saw a man collapse at a zebra crossing: one moment walking, and then on the ground in a heap. People immediately rushed around him. Whatever help he needed I hope he got. Or whatever end came for him I hope was swift. In truth, that's the way I'd most like to go. The drawn-out, slow passing that people like Odette and Chris had, that terrifies me. Uncle Steve and his dreadful time with oesophageal cancer – I can't imagine a worse nightmare. To this day I can't get a scratchy throat without feeling a chill run through me.

I know how I want it to be. Of course, this isn't how it will be, but if I had my choice then I'd be sitting in the comfy corner of the sofa with a good book – one I am hopefully just finishing, as I'd hate to miss the end of a well-told story. Good music would be playing in the background. A dog or three would be curled up with me, snoring. There'd be pictures of kids and grandkids and weddings and holidays around the room. I don't think I'll make it to great-grandchildren. Mel will. The women in her family live to be ninety-seven, and then gravity catches them. It's not the case for the men in my family. Late seventies, maybe mid-eighties.

The sofa, a book, some kind of nice white blanket, ideally knitted for me by a grandchild or wife. Mel will read that part and snort, but it's my daydream so I'm keeping it. It took my wife over four years to knit me a scarf once, so a blanket is never going to happen. I'll sit there safe, warm and loved, and then I'll just slip away. I know this leaves the chaos of discovery and an ambulance and paperwork, but for that moment, that peaceful moment, it seems ideal.

To be there and then ... gone.

Finger still in a book, ideally pointing at the words *The End*.

~

Yes, I know that the way I'd want to go is not the only question about death. People want to know: how does working so closely with death affect my life? Have I learnt to seize the day and control my temper and drink less and dance more? The answer to all is no.

I do have a far fuller appreciation of the fact that death can come at any moment. Any morning could be the last morning for any of us. I could pop out one morning for a coffee and never come back – be whisked off in an ambulance to be pronounced dead and on my way to the coroners before my bed has cooled.

Do I appreciate life more? I love life, but lazily. Years ago, before funeral directing, Mel found out I had never been on a roller-coaster as I knew I would hate it.

'But how do you know you would hate it?'

'Because I know I would.'

Unfortunately, this conversation was on a New Year's Eve, and I ended up promising to say yes to everything for a year. Almost immediately I was riding an actual roller-coaster, and I hated it. I went camping and suffered the indignities of that. Awful art exhibitions (I like pictures of car parks and alleyways, and that's about it), and so many barbecues with the in-laws that I would normally have hidden from. At the end of the year Mel said how great it had been and asked how it had been for me.

'Awful,' I said. 'So are you going to say yes to all of my ideas for a year now?'

Mel looked at me and said, 'Shit, no.'

Since moving into death and seeing so closely that life really can end any moment, I respect serenity much more. I carve out an hour or so every Saturday to read. I collect awful jokes to tell the kids. I cook the things I see on Instagram. Make sauerkraut. Cure egg yolks. Pickle rhubarb.

Mel and I recently started walking the dog every morning at 5am in a vague 'nudging fifty get healthy' way and I'm loving the quiet start before work, the half-hour with just the two of us while the dog skips around without a care in the world. The dog has it right: play when playing is good, and then rest, relax, eat and drink.

Reducing the stress in the world: I think that is what I have learnt. Irrespective of HSC results, my kids are going to be twenty-five, forty-five, sixty-five years old and hopefully happy. Irrespective of the time taken to stress about it, I'll die one day, but thus far it hasn't been this day, so maybe I'll see what the kids are when they are twenty-five and forty-five. Likely not sixty-five, but I bet they are still beautiful.

The other question people have for funeral directors is whether we have any insights about what happens after death. For me, from an atheist viewpoint, I find the idea of there being nothing on the other side tremendously reassuring. Heaven I find to be a frightening idea; eternity seems utterly appalling. Every day is such a swarm of activity and thought and motion – life is so full to brimming – that I honestly feel that after all that, the candle flame simply flickering out is correct.

If I'm wrong, then I'll figure that out then.

Finally, working closely with grief, at least in my case, brings all your feelings closer to the surface. I'm very aware that I am an easy mark for sad movies and books. I carry a mostly full bucket of emotion, and the slightest blue moment on television will lead to my daughter saying, 'Dad, are you crying?'

After a recent funeral – and a huge hug from the partner of the deceased – I got home and watched *The Iron Giant* with the kids for no other reason than that I knew the end would uncork the bottle and let out the tears that I was holding in.

I've learnt that a good cry is as healthy as laughing riotously around a fire-pit with friends and whisky. Both keep me in balance.

Teaching Florists

I held the door open and invited her inside.

'Inside?' she asked.

I smiled and said yes.

She shook her head. 'I don't think so.'

'But aren't you here for the class?'

'The class?'

I started to feel a little like Jareth in the movie *Labyrinth*.

'Yes, the class. The floristry class, in the funeral home.'

She nodded yes and said, 'But I don't want to come in alone.'

'To the funeral home?'

She smiled now. 'I guess I'm being silly.'

I stepped out and closed the door behind me and sat on the low wall out the front. 'Not at all,' I said. 'It's rare people come here without something terrible having happened. To be coming here for a class in funeral flowers isn't a normal day.'

She was the first florist arriving. More would come soon.

'I was at a funeral the other day,' I told her, 'and a chap arrived just as our service was drawing near to starting. He rushed to sign in, but we checked, "Are you here for the such-and-such service sir?" He wasn't – he was at the wrong chapel and the wrong crematorium. There are two almost side by side, and it happens so often. People come to the wrong crematorium and almost miss their funeral. Anyway, I told him he would still make it if he went back to his car. Just 200 yards further down the road, and he'd be there. Then he told us that he'd come by bus, and there was no way he'd make it in time.'

She sipped her takeaway coffee and sat on the wall beside me.

'I asked him if he minded going to a funeral in a hearse, and he said he didn't mind at all. I waved over my driver and asked him to run the gentleman to the other crematorium and said I'd look after things here. The chap jumped into the hearse, and I can only imagine now that he has a dinner-party story for the ages – the day he went to the wrong crematorium and hitched a ride in a hearse to a funeral.'

She laughed, and another florist turned the corner and nervously stepped towards the door.

'Ready to come in now?' I asked.

She nodded.

~

We held a class for florists every six months as part of their training. They would come for a morning at our funeral home, meet the boss and then be led through a three-hour talk on funerals, traditions and, most importantly for them, flowers. This included things like how long they'd typically have to prepare the flowers before a funeral, the traditions of different religions – no flowers for Jewish, more flowers than you can imagine for Greek – space restrictions in hearses, coffin-top dimensions and so on. The end of the session would be an open Q&A, where they could ask us absolutely anything.

Before the class arrived, we would set things up as for any chapel service, ticking off the first-impression essentials of a funeral home. We lit a scented candle, so the whiff of sandalwood would be there in the background. We lit a few more candles on the round tables outside the chapel, and the artificial candles were turned on in their sconces behind where the coffin would sit.

Candlelight is seen as peaceful and respectful, but to me it's a controlled chaos. Take that candle out to the dry woods or set it under the bed or sofa and the flame will devour everything. Unchecked grief will overwhelm just like fire. The candles, flickering there, to me were reminders of grief burning as it should – held and tended.

In the background we always have music. Handel and his *Water Music* if we can think of nothing else, but often a mix of John Williams and Sigur Rós.

We put out bowls of chocolates on each table. Grief burns blood sugar, and a piece of chocolate or two can be a great relief.

Then, for the florists, we have an empty coffin in place, on a trolley. A chance to see, to touch, to know the size and shape of the coffin where their flowers may one day sit.

We have the hearse parked at the side of the chapel, reversed in, out of the way – and often unnoticed until we point it out to the class.

~

Gradually the room fills. Twenty faces are scattered among the pews. These florists have chosen to sit like any good group of strangers – politely at a distance from each other.

I've often noticed this distanced way that people choose to sit at a funeral. During most Christian funeral services, there is a moment called 'the sign of peace', during which attendees are encouraged to turn and shake hands and say 'Peace be with you'. One priest we work with often introduces it by saying, 'This is the moment that none of you like – and I can tell by the way you are sitting.' We watch from the back; if there is anyone who has sat too far from the others to manage a handshake, I walk over and shake hands with them.

The boss takes the floor and welcomes the florists. She introduces herself and me. She introduces the funeral home, talks about how long it has existed, how she's the fifth generation since the original owner. She talks about how we will be touching on death – a subject not often spoken about in day-to-day life.

'Death is triggering,' she says, 'and if anyone in the room feels discomforted, please let us know. We will look after you. It's hard to even walk into a funeral home.' I see heads nod. 'It is hard. It can be one of the hardest walks a person can make.'

She hands over to me, and we start talking about what a funeral home does. We do funerals, of course, but also pre-paid funerals, where people can lock everything in decades before their death. We also do pre-arranged funerals, where people come and talk it all through, write it all down, but possibly don't pay anything – just have their wishes documented. We offer community services: we have held talks for nursing home staff on late-life organ donation and sexuality in retirement homes. We also have a justice of the peace on the premises – if ever you can't find one, your local funeral home will have one.

We talk about the ownership of a funeral – who has the right to arrange a funeral. I put a hypothetical situation up on the screen:

A young girl dies suddenly. Her parents are divorced. Her mother comes in to arrange the funeral with us. The following day her father makes contact and wants to take the funeral elsewhere. Who has the rights?

Florists tend to be female, and there is a swing to the mother of the deceased as having the rights. Then discussion starts and, after a few moments, someone asks, 'Who did she live with?'

The answer: the father. As such, he has the rights to arrange the funeral. The parent with whom the child is living has the control. Obviously, we hope for communication in these circumstances, for the parts of a split family to unite. We try to remain the calm island in a storm, should one develop.

A second hypothetical:

A young man dies suddenly. The mother comes to see us with his partner. The partner sits quietly as the mother makes the arrangements. The following day, the partner calls wanting to change the arrangements. Who has the rights?

They are much quicker in this instance. A relationship that has lasted more than six months is considered de facto, and a partner has the rights to lead the arrangements. We try to balance both sides, given the young man will have been a son for far longer than he has been a partner, and we hope both sides can work together. We can often find ourselves in turbulent waters, which is another reason why we move slowly, carefully, and remain calm. Tolstoy's *Anna Karenina* saves me here: 'Happy families are all alike; every unhappy family is unhappy in its own way.' I've quoted that line in so many meetings now, and people seem surprised that their unique family tension was summed up in the nineteenth century.

An executor is the highest authority. If there are multiple executors, then we have to hope they are in agreement. If two executors disagree, a funeral cannot proceed and, at a certain point, we have to step away.

After an executor comes the spouse or domestic partner. Domestic partner means precisely that, irrespective of gender. We still find in same-sex relationships that a partner may be spoken of as a 'special friend' by the parents, but less often now. Love and loss are the same, irrespective of sexuality. It's wonderful to love, it is painful to lose, and funerals are becoming far more human in that sense. Thankfully, it has been a good few years now since I last heard eulogies along the lines of 'and thanks to his special friend, who was with him through the hard times'.

Children of the deceased come next in arrangement authority – wide-eyed and frightened, even if they are in their fifties. Losing a grandparent is natural; it's expected. It's almost a rite of passage – a moment where we stand a little taller and take on a little more of life. Losing a parent, that's a jolt. The person we've always turned to for guidance and warmth and reassurance – they can't be gone. At heart, we are all still kids, it's just the reflection in the mirror that changes. Once our parents are gone, we are recast as adults and are aware that we are now closer to our own passing.

Parents of the deceased are the next. If there is no executor, partner or child, then the parents take the lead. If this is the case, then things are brittle. A parent arranging their child's funeral is an upside-down circumstance. Bitterly unnatural, fragile and overwhelming. Every word is a blow. Naming the date of birth brings tears. The word 'ashes' lands with a heavy thud. The hardest question I have to ask when a parent calls regarding the loss of a child, whatever age that child may be, is 'What is their name?'

After these, in the order of authority are grandparents, aunts and uncles, before, finally the state takes over.

In describing this list to the florists, I stress the importance of an executor – the person who will handle your affairs for you, and whom you trust to honour the wishes that you have made.

Then I ask them all, 'Why do we have a funeral? What purpose does it serve?'

One of the florists will answer that we have to do something with the body. A death certificate from Births, Deaths and Marriages will not come until the body has reached its final stage – be it cremation or burial.

We talk about cremated remains. People imagine these as paper ashes like burnt birthday cards, but they aren't, they are grittier and heavy.

We talk about the limitations and expense of burial, with fewer and fewer graves remaining, and prices ever-increasing. Older graves have an issue of lineage, especially when the original rite-holders of the plot are long since passed. For a great-uncle to be buried in a cemetery plot to which he is attached by lineage, the cemetery would need complete lineage and statutory declarations from all surviving relatives before they could permit it. Gaining all of this paperwork can feel like Dickens's Jarndyce v Jarndyce case in *Bleak House*.

A younger florist may ask about bodies being dissolved in water, or freeze dried and turned to compost, or buried in planting sacks for trees to grow from. The dissolving of a deceased person is now available in Australia, but it's very limited in availability and as yet far from a common practice. For now, I can only steer people towards burial or cremation. There is a handbook for burial at sea but it's not a book I have had to look to as yet.

I ask the florists if they think of interment as being underground, then explain that one can also be interred in a mausoleum. In these instances, the deceased needs to be embalmed. I've placed bodies in crypts and mausoleums that will be lying there, unchanged, as I grow steadily wider and greyer, year by year.

Sometimes a florist will say, 'I'm leaving my body to science.'

'Great,' I say, and then ask if science knows.

If science doesn't know about you, then science can't take you.

'I'm leaving myself to the body farm for forensics.'

The same question applies: if forensics researchers don't know about your wish, then they can't take you. It's one thing to say 'may science learn from my cold, dead yet fascinating body', but if science is unaware, then chances are science will say no.

Organ donation I adore. If a family tells me a relative died in an accident but is with the hospital for organ donation at this time, I have to hold back from hugging them. How many lives may be improved from receiving the organs of someone taken too soon? Truly, if you can, then do. Tell your family this is your wish. Make sure that they know. Of course, organ donation doesn't take everything, but what can be taken enhances – or saves – a life, and truly, what better eulogy for someone than 'in his death he saved a dozen lives'?

When Tilda was going into surgery, Mel and I spoke about it. Should things go badly, would we? Mel said of course we would – if things went wrong, then absolutely – and then we dismissed that concept as one not to dwell on.

~

Beyond the physical reason for a funeral, though, comes the spiritual. We are becoming less religious as a society, yet there is a still a lean towards tradition – towards what has been done for thousands of years.

This might be a Catholic mass, with its prayer and communion, organ and hymns, stained glass and glory. A service in a cathedral with the resonance and the sheer scale of things reducing us all to children in a master's house. Prayers and readings delivered in the same way as when our great-great-great-grandparents were young. Possibly the only change being that now some of the churches have AV screens and sound systems. Communion is offered, incense is burnt, holy water is splashed over the coffin. History happens over and again, the same words spoken, often in the same church. With flowers: flowers on the coffin, flowers in bowls to the side of the coffin, wreathes, bunches, flowers everywhere.

Or it could be an Anglican service in one of the many beautiful old churches, or High Anglican services, with such spectacle as to swarm the senses with colour and sound and leave the attendees almost overwhelmed with grandeur – and flowers, again everywhere, every colour, every scent.

Or it could be a Jewish service, with its simplicity and emphasis on community. One of the most humbling things I've ever seen was at a Jewish service. A parent whose child had passed was sitting at the front. Behind them, a crowd of friends and family reached forward to touch the shoulders of grief, and if not those shoulders, then the shoulders of those close by, and further back, creating a momentary human circuit of support and love that, even in the midst of tragedy, completely took my breath away. We look after Jewish cremation, should it be required, or a burial if the deceased is to be placed in unconsecrated ground – a Jewish wife buried beside a Catholic husband, perhaps. No flowers, though, except for an occasional single rose or simple bunch.

It could be a Buddhist service, with deep chanting, to the point that my mind seems to separate from the moment and slip into such colour and beauty as to be like the ending of the movie *2001: A Space Odyssey*. I find these services so enriching. By the end you feel brighter and coloured in where before you were outline only.

So far I have no experience of a Muslim funeral service, but I have the number of the people who do. Should a family call us, uncertain where to go, we can direct them on.

In whatever way the spirit of the deceased is honoured, a funeral home assists. Atheist services replace 'spirit' with the word 'memory'. The memory of dad lives on. Mum's memory will be with me. Memory is the sadness and the beauty here, as no new memories will be formed now that they are gone. In speaking of them, though – in listening to the memories – we still learn new things about people we have known all our lives.

Then I speak to the florists about the emotional reason for a funeral.

It is the day we stamp in the calendar to say, 'Today is the day I am not okay. It is the day I am missing my mother.' Grief hides itself most of the time these days, we give it a week or so and then expect people back at work, back on deck and functional. We are so busy, so needed, so essential, that we struggle to convince even ourselves that we simply must stop and grieve. A funeral is a declaration of that need. *Emotionally, I do not wish to be here today, I would rather be anywhere else, but I am here, and I am sad, and I need support.*

The days of black armbands to show we are still grieving have gone. Now, people are shy of someone coming over and saying, 'Are you okay?' – which to me is ridiculous. People who come to see me insist they are okay, and I remind them that it is more than okay *not* to be okay. 'I won't cry at the funeral,' I'm told often. Cry at funerals! Everyone there loves you – let it out!

Finally, there is the social aspect of a funeral. How many times, at weddings or funerals, have you heard someone say, 'I haven't seen you since ...' We lose contact with people as we age, until we only see them at funerals, but seeing them makes us younger again. The memory of the deceased friend unites us and, despite being under the cloud of loss, we can speak of brighter, better and younger times.

~

Our florists now know the reasons for funerals and who can plan one, and we move on to everything funeral directors need to know.

The Births, Deaths and Marriages information: parents' information, marriage history, children of the deceased, where they were born, a *rat-a-tat* of personal questions that lead to a flurry of phone calls to siblings or cousins for 'grandma's maiden name' or 'grandad's job'.

The coffin: particle board or solid timber or even cardboard. Hessian sacks aren't allowed as yet, though people ask for them regularly.

The venue: church, chapel, bowling club, bar, back garden, front garden, lounge room. I've wheeled in coffins and placed them beside the sofa and television in the lounge room. Carried them to the back garden for one last morning tea with the family. Brought them to front gardens for the same, but with a view of the ocean. I've even stopped in a driveway for a son to say a few brief words over his dad's coffin before we took him on for cremation.

And then all the other questions.

Will we be running newspaper notices?

Are we developing a slideshow for the family or will they provide one?

Is there music we can download for them?

Or do we need live music? A violinist? Guitarist? Trumpets? Are we having a *Star Wars* fanfare in church? Do we need a choir? A band? A bagpiper? Do they need rehearsal time?

Do we need an Auslan interpreter for any deaf family members?

A family advised us their relative had loved dogs more than people, so we ran a notice in the paper inviting the dogs of Bondi. We had bowls and dog treats and an open door to any passing pet to come in. Another family had the funeral timed to a favourite talkback radio show of the deceased, and a small radio played on top of the coffin during the service.

Balloons? Doves?

Shots of whisky, vodka, brandy, slivovitz? Served beside the coffin or from the coffin top itself. Brandy at the graveside for all attendees of the burial. Champagne during a slideshow of the person's life.

Is the hearse to travel via a certain route – family homes, work locations?

Anything and everything that we could possibly help with.

'That's a lot,' a florist will say.

I agree, and then point to the last item on the list.

Flowers.

'This isn't to say flowers are our last thought, but that they are one of many things we need to lock into place. With a wedding, people plan for months prior to the event. With a funeral here in Sydney, if you pass away on a Saturday, your funeral is likely to be on the following Friday or perhaps early the week after. There's not much time for us to get a lot in place.'

Now we are on flowers, though, I suggest we ask: why flowers? Why do we have them at a funeral at all? Archaeologists have found articles dating back eleven thousand years that show flowers being placed with bodies in burial rituals. Why? We don't know. During the plague – the black death – pockets of posies were carried to mask the smell of death. Could it be why ancient Egyptians placed the herb rosemary with mummified bodies? The florists frown, and I point out that this scent would also cover the smell of the body.

Then we show images of Lady Diana's tributes in London, or Martin Place in Sydney after the Lindt Café siege.

Flowers everywhere. Why?

When people don't know what else to do, flowers give us a sense that we have helped to take away the stain of death. Flowers are beautiful, ever-growing and joyful. Often the first thing people say as they arrive at a funeral is, 'Oh, she would have loved the flowers,' or 'Aren't those just beautiful?' Flowers are an icebreaker – something to say beyond the dreadful fact of why people are gathering, that someone has died.

Roses are the most used flower. Single stems are thrown into the grave, casket cover arrangements of them sit atop the coffin. Some cultures see chrysanthemums as representing grief and sorrow (whereas I see them as the flower I flat-out cannot pronounce, being gifted as I am with a lisp). Poppies are a symbol of wartime and are used at RSL services. Lillies are seen as the flower of death, though one minister we knew was violently allergic to them, so we would tend to intervene if a family wanted lilies at his church. Orchids mean simply 'I will always love you'. Hyacinths can be taken to mean 'you are in my prayers'. Hydrangeas many believe to show true and essential emotions.

We transpose meaning onto flowers, and meaning reassures us. The flowers are beautiful at a time when beauty seems to have been taken. A Chinese family will fill our chapel with flowers, colour and clamour everywhere. A Greek family once required two hearses – the second to move all the flowers that were brought by mourners to the service. Flowers say simply, and loudly, 'I know, and I am sorry. For the colour that is now gone from your life, I offer this.'

The florists like that part.

~

We give them tips for dealing with grieving customers. Grief is erratic. It steals sleep and suppresses hunger and leaves us adrift from our usual clarity and gravity.

We tell the florists to be clear, be slow and repeat things. Let the customer take their time, let them express themselves. Encourage the client to bring a support person with them. We always ask, 'And will somebody be with you when we meet?' Write everything down. We give clients a copy of everything: words said out loud are easily forgotten, and having them written down is a reassurance. We encourage our florists to be understanding – grieving families often change their minds. They call us to change coffins, viewing times, images in slideshows. We have brief, intense relationships with these families, and supporting every changing request is a small thing to do if it helps. Lastly, we tell the florists to follow up with communications. Call to say, 'Now, what we said is … and what we will do is …'

Most clearly, though, we tell them not to take it personally if grief turns to anger when they are dealing with a client.

I've had one sentence in a meeting trigger a huge response. I said simply, 'Now, we need to consider a coffin,' and within seconds the man across the table from me had kicked his chair away and was reaching out for me. Swinging his right fist and missing by only inches. The sentence had shattered whatever defences he had left, and the mere suggestion of a coffin for his loved one was a consideration too much. It rendered me as the person responsible for this pain. I pushed my chair back and stood up as he stared at me, wild-eyed and determined. His family held his arms, and I asked if we should take a break. 'It's okay,' I said, as they started to apologise. 'Honestly, it's okay.'

It wasn't okay; my heart was hammering. I haven't been in a physical fight since school. Much as I love violent cinema, I find immediate violence and aggression right in front of me extremely disturbing. Death is even more disturbing, though, and my feelings were not important in this situation. I simply repeated that it was all okay, and we took a break for ten minutes.

'It won't be that bad for you,' we tell the florists.

~

I tell them all the things we have had in place of flowers. Blankets, favourite quilts, covers or clothing. Laid across the coffin and reclaimed at the end of the service. Taxidermised pets are sat like sentries beside the nameplate. Cremated pets in small ash containers: smaller sentries there on the surface. Trophies – sporting triumphs still boasted about. Chess sets. Cigars. Vegetables. Buckets of river water. Bottles of whisky, of vodka or home-brew. Radios chattering away. If it has meaning, then it should be there.

Then we move to the coffin to the front and we ask, 'Have you ever seen inside a coffin?' There's a shiver and a ripple and a few muted yesses. I lift the lid, asking the boss briefly, 'This one is empty, yes?'

I invite them forward. We gather around the coffin and talk through the size and the shape. We talk about how a casket is oblong and a coffin is tapered. We show them the lining and, after a pause, they start to touch and move around the coffin. Things become easier. Someone will say it looks quite comfortable. Every time, someone asks if they can lie in it – or would that be weird?

We show them the hearse and the space available. If the coffin has a raised lid (which is a lid that arches a bit higher when it is closed), then we only have *this* much remaining room for safe clearance on the flowers. Talk to your funeral director, we tell them, and make sure things will fit.

~

After the hearse, we move back inside and open the floor up to questions. Any questions, I say. I promise you won't shock us.

They don't burn the coffin, do they?

Yes, they do. If they didn't, I say to them, imagine what it would be like for the poor staff at the crematorium placing bodies directly into the cremator. They'd be in therapy every day. The coffin is cremated, leaving a trace of coffin in the ashes.

Is it true that pacemakers can explode?

They do, and you never want to be the funeral home that caused an explosion at the crematorium. Great care is taken to determine if there is a pacemaker – families are asked, doctors confirm, and our mortuary attendant visually checks.

Do you – you know – really dress the dead? Don't you just throw the clothing in when it's a closed casket?

No, we dress everybody for whom we are given clothing. If no clothing is provided, then we wash the clothing the person came to us in and redress them in that, or we place a cover over them that ensures that, from the neck down, they have full dignity. Right up until the very last second, you can ask to see them – after all, they are yours. Yes, it's unusual, dressing the dead, but it's also peaceful, methodical and strangely satisfying once they are fully clothed, with tie knotted and shoes laced.

Hair keeps growing after death, doesn't it?

No, I'm afraid not. After we die, we dehydrate, and our hair and fingernails just appear to be longer because our skin retracts slightly.

Are you scared of dying?

No. Interestingly, most people list public speaking as more terrifying than dying, so in that sense, you'd all rather be there in the coffin than standing here talking to a bunch of terrifying florists. Seriously, though, no – I'm not afraid. I'm afraid of pain, of sudden events or drowning or calamity, as we all are. The idea of death, though, honestly, I find it quite reassuring. I'd rather it waited a good long time, but once the lights go out, I don't think I am afraid of that. Life is the longest thing that we do; it makes sense to me that it has to have an ending. It would terrify me if it didn't.

Have you ever, you know, seen a ghost?

This is where my wife's voice says, 'Of course you haven't.' But she's not here right now, so … One Saturday I was in the old office on my own, sorting some work. It's not unusual to come in on a weekend if you're on call. Sometimes it's easier to just chip away at this or take care of that. I was working through something when I heard a door behind me click.

I called out 'Hi', as a few of my colleagues lived above the funeral home.

No one answered.

The nearest door was the door to the viewing room, where families would sit with their loved ones. I glanced up to see the door still closed, but then in front of it, for maybe a second or six, there was and there wasn't an outline or a solid figure of a man in a hat and coat with a full beard, walking slowly but staying in the same place, his head slowly turning, and his arms and legs moving. He was solidly there but stubbornly not there. And then he absolutely wasn't there. He wasn't there because he was just ripples of sunlight on the white wall, and he wasn't there because Mel would tell me he wasn't there. I don't believe he was there at all, but I saw him.

I don't tell the florists this. I tell them our mortician sometimes talks of the radio skipping around one day, finding the same song on different channels for the duration of the time she was working on a body. They're generally happy with that version of a ghost story.

Do you lay coins on the eyes of the dead?

No. One body I was putting away after a viewing had the most furious look on his face. The family had said he had seemed so at peace, but to me he seemed irate, as though he was about to burst into invective and berate me. As I closed the coffin, I honestly expected something to happen, the face was so contorted into rage. I don't tell them this, though. I tell them we put fake money in or on the coffin sometimes.

Once, at a graveside, a family had fake money, paper clothing, paper hats and paper telephones, all of which they dropped onto the coffin. Joyous handfuls of decorative money spiralling down to the coffin.

Is it creepy here at night?

No, I don't think so. I've been here at night quite a few times, and it's only creepy if you start telling yourself it should be. The ticks and clicks and taps and groans are just the building being old. If you start thinking about it, though, then yes, it becomes creepy. Anywhere does, though, doesn't it? At night anything familiar can take on a malevolence all of its own.

What does embalming mean?

Technically, it means to preserve from decay. I've watched a few embalms now and it's quite fascinating, if your mind looks at it that way. It's not my place to describe the process, and I would only get it wrong if I did. Suffice it to say that the times I have seen it done, it has been done with skill, care, patience and almost artistry. The human body is quite amazing. For the period that it is our own, I think we forget quite how complex and astonishing we are.

Can I have a ride in a hearse?

Every time we have ever run the class someone asks this. The only answer I can give is that you can have a ride in a hearse, no problem – just not today. One day, though, one day you will.

Have you ever seen someone die?

No, I haven't. I've arrived not long after and found people still warm in their bed, looking for all the world like they are asleep. But no, I have not been there as the last breath was drawn in. The last breath coming out, though, I've felt that on my cheek many times.

~

The florists pack their bags and say thank you and fill out their questionnaire. Most of the time, these are full of appreciation and ten out of tens. Except one time, when one attendee wrote, 'The trainer was too macho.'

Quietly, I still wear this as something I am quite proud of.

Meetings

During renovations of our new premises, we had a temporary arrangement room rented a few doors down from our office. We'd make a time with the family, and then direct them to meet us at a different address, explaining that we were going through building works. I'd go and stand outside the door to this room up to twenty minutes ahead of time, as people had a habit of being wildly early or extremely late. Standing there in a shirt and tie by the open door was a pretty clear sign that this was the room they were heading towards. Meanwhile, dogs would wander up and I'd stroke their heads, and locals would make the same joke over and over: 'You're looking for the dead on the street now?'

On this particular day I was waiting on a woman who was eager to cremate a relative.

'Wish I could have done it while he was alive,' she'd told me by phone.

'I'm sorry that we couldn't help you sooner,' I'd replied.

She'd snorted a laugh, and I'd said I'd see her at 10am and given her the address.

'Why's that different to your office?'

I explained the building works and general chaos in our office.

'So, who will be there?'

I said just myself and her. There was a long silence.

'Okay,' she said.

On the dot at 10am, a woman strode towards me. Leather jacket, skinny jeans and tied-back hair. She looked at me and asked, 'Richard?' I said her name back. I gestured inside, and she peered through the door and slowly stepped in. I came in after her and locked the door.

'Why are you doing that?' she asked.

'Just so we aren't interrupted – postmen, people looking for the jewellery store that used to be here, that sort of thing. Would you rather I left it unlocked?'

She nodded sharply, two quick bobs of her head.

I unlocked the door and took a seat at the table.

'You seem uncomfortable. Is there anything I can do?'

She crossed her legs and pushed her chair back a little, so she wasn't hemmed in. She glanced at the door and then back at me.

'I have a knife, a big one, so don't try anything, okay?' she said.

I was holding my pen above the file.

'Okay,' I said.

'I'm serious,' she whispered, her hand hovering over her bag.

'I'm sorry, I don't have anyone I can invite to join us. I should have thought of this before. But, look, if it would make you feel more comfortable, would you like to take the knife out and hold it?'

She stared at me, her eyes hard. From her bag, she pulled out a folded knife that she opened out. It had a long, serrated blade coming from a black grip that she held defensively in her hand.

'Better?'

She looked from the blade to me and back again, then nodded.

'Okay, so now I need to ask a few questions.'

We worked through the file, and she held onto the knife throughout. When it came time to sign the paperwork, I put asterisks by each line she had to sign and stepped away from the table to the small kitchenette so she could pick up the pen with her knife hand and sign. She read and shouted out a few questions to me, and then signed her name.

'All good?' I called.

She said it was.

I came back through and found her now standing, still holding the knife.

'Thank you,' I said. 'I would imagine we will have cremation arranged by Thursday. I'll call you when I have a firm date and time. I'd normally shake your hand at this point but ...' I nodded to the knife.

She smiled a diagonal grin and nodded. 'Yeah, I don't like handshakes.'

'Truth be told, neither do I. I've got ridiculously small hands,' I told her, waving my hands in the air. She watched them and nodded.

'Man, you really do. For a big fella, that seems a bit wrong.'

She put the knife away. I don't know if it was my hands or the meeting being over, but she smiled at me once more and turned and left, the door clicking shut behind her.

I sat down, pulling my file together and the signed pages she had left me. Her chair was still out, her water bottle half finished. She'd been sitting there throughout, holding a knife, wound up enough that, had I sneezed, I would probably be bleeding out right now.

I shuddered a little, and then locked up and went back to the office. I walked in to the sounds of sawing and hammering and builders shouting.

'Arrange go okay?' a colleague asked me.

'Yeah. It was a bit of a first, she held a knife on me the whole time.'

He stared at me. 'You know you shouldn't have stayed there, right? I mean, that is not right.'

I couldn't disagree with him. It wasn't right. I shouldn't have sat there with her holding a knife. I should have ended the meeting as soon as she even said the word knife. Instead, I'd said she could hold it if it made her feel better, and it had seemed to. I guess that was all that seemed to matter at the time.

~

At another meeting, a man in his mid-thirties had come to plan his own funeral. He was answering my questions quickly, and very sharply. He wasn't terminally ill or suffering in any way, he said, he simply wanted 'my affairs in order.' He was dressed in an imitation of smart – a shirt that wasn't buttoned properly and a tie that was clashing in colour. Black jeans and brown shoes. We'd been through all the personal information, and then what he wanted in a service – coffin in our chapel, a female celebrant, he'd get back to me on music. For flowers, 'Well, I dunno, Aussie natives?' I'd costed things out for him and suggested he take some time to think about it. There was no hurry – the plan we had drawn up could stay on file for years, there was really no need to pay right now.

'Is there anything you want to ask me? Anything we haven't covered?' I asked.

He nodded. 'After I die, what happens?'

The question wasn't unusual.

'Well, we're talking a long time hence. But should you die in hospital, we would collect you once the medical paperwork is in order. Should you die in a nursing home, then it's the same situation, but we attend a little quicker, as nursing homes often don't have cool storerooms. Should you die at home, then, if no doctor can come and issue a medical cause of death, we would bring you into care from the coroners after they have confirmed nothing untoward occurred.'

He was shaking his head. 'No, I mean, after I die and I am in your care, what happens then?'

'Oh, I see. Well, if by then you have a pacemaker, then we would have to remove it. Beyond that, we would wash you, and dress you if there are any clothes provided for you.'

'Who does that?' he sat forward and put his hands on his knees.

'Our mortuary attendant.'

He nodded as though this was all good and proper. He shuffled the file in front of him, where I'd put some notes, and then he looked back at me.

'This mortuary attendant, are they male or female?'

'Our mortuary attendant is a female.'

He sighed. Nodded. Clucked his tongue on the roof of his mouth.

'Would you – do you – I mean, could I – do you have a photograph of them? The female?'

I shook my head. 'No. I'm afraid not.'

He was fidgeting now. 'Are they on your website? Could I look there?'

I shook my head.

'Can I ask, what do you mean by wash me?' He was beginning to bite his bottom lip and his eyes were looking distant. 'How do they wash me?'

'We wash all of our clients. Everyone who comes our way is treated with dignity and respect.'

He nodded and made 'uhm' sounds. 'So, she would wash ... all of me?'

I didn't reply but sat in the silence for the moment.

'She would wash, I mean, me.' He grinned, his cheeks going red.

I pulled my mobile phone from my pocket and faked a call, saying, 'Yes, yes, I understand,' and then placed it face-down on the table.

'I'm sorry, my friend, that was my son's school. I'm going to have to end this meeting. Take some time and have a think about things, and if you want me to draw up the contracts, let me know and we'll meet again. Call any time at all if I can help.'

He stood awkwardly.

'I – I – just want to know more about the washing. Does she wear gloves?'

I held the door for him. 'I'm sorry, my friend, I really have to go.'

He nodded and walked away quickly, head down as he moved along the street, swiftly blending into the pedestrians as just another person going about just another day. I've never heard from him again.

~

'I'm going to try and die next Wednesday.'

'I'm sorry?'

The woman I was meeting with winced and nodded. 'I have to go in for a check-up, I'll try and die there and then. Less mess. No one has to find me.'

We were working through a pre-paid cremation at her home. Her lights were out, a fuse blown somewhere.

'Well, don't try too hard, okay?'

She waved me off with a sharp *pffft* sound. 'It'll be easier all round.'

I looked around the apartment. A tiny table, tiny television, tiny kitchenette, and a dark hallway to a tiny bedroom and tiny bathroom.

'Look, I'm sure if I can find the fuse box, I can get your lights back on.'

She waved me away again. 'No point.'

There were books on the table by the television, but they had a layer of dust on them. She saw me looking.

'I gave up on them, didn't care how they ended. Take them if you want.'

I shook my head and put my file away.

'Are you sure I can't do anything? I'm sure I can flick the fuse.'

She waved me off again. 'Do you have everything you need to know?'

I stood and nodded. 'Short of the lottery numbers, I guess I'm fine.'

'Lottery is for fools,' she said.

I agreed, though there was pressure at work to join a jackpot syndicate.

I held out my hand. 'Take care,' I said.

She nodded. 'Next Wednesday,' she said again and turned back to her shadows.

The following Thursday, I got a call; she'd died the day before.

Things Said Towards the End

Legend holds that King George V sung the praises of an English seaside town, Bognor Regis, on his deathbed. His doctor leant towards him as he was in his final throes and said, 'Your majesty, remember Bognor,' as an effort to bring happier times to mind for the dying king. The king replied with a sigh and an exclamation of, 'Ah, Bognor!' and then died. The legend changes, though, with some reports having the king dying after exclaiming, 'Bugger Bognor!' His physician's diary records that his last words were 'God damn you'.

I don't hear the last words of the deceased in my care, arriving as I do after the fact. Often, though, I have heard things said as that last corner approaches, when death is in sight. Maybe as he starts to rise and reaches out his hand.

~

I was transcribing a woman's information for her pre-paid funeral service. I asked her the same questions we always ask: the ones that

Births, Deaths and Marriages need answers to in order to generate a death certificate. With a pre-paid funeral arrangement, we gather this information when we meet the client and then a year, five years, ten years later, when they pass, we verify the information we took with the family. I had listed this woman's date of birth, occupation during life, marriage history ('too damn many of those, you'd have thought I'd have learnt after the third one but no, I just love falling in love').

Then she smiled and nodded to *Date of Death*. 'I already died, you know?'

I paused and looked at her. 'You look well.'

'It was a car crash,' she said. 'I was driving.'

'I'm glad you're okay.'

'I was dead for over twenty minutes, they tell me.'

'I don't think I've ever done a pre-paid funeral for someone who has already died once.'

She frowned and thought about it. 'Do I get a discount? Having already died once?'

'I'll see what I can do.'

'So, I was dead. Twenty minutes dead. Do you know what I saw?'

I put my pen down and settled back in the chair.

'Light. Such perfect light. It was rich and deep and warm. I was walking towards it. Someone was holding my hand, and we were walking away from the car and the shattered glass. We were walking, and I saw inside the light my mother, my grandmother, my father, all holding their hands out to me.' She was smiling. 'You don't believe me, do you?'

'I want to, but it's a big leap to take.'

'Someone led me nearly all the way in, and then we stopped, and I knew it wasn't my time. Standing there, in this light, I kissed my mother. And then I was back. On Earth. Broken arm. Broken leg. Alive.'

Her eyes were wet now, and I reached over and held her hand.

'You don't believe me?'

'I know you believe the story. And that's enough. I want it to be true, very much. Just for now I have bills to pay and soccer boots to buy for my son and weight to try and lose and a dog that keeps leaving puddles in the laundry.'

'Life. In all its colours.'

'That's where I am, yes.'

'Death is colourful too. It's beautiful.' She smiled with such certainty.

'Well, not yet, okay?' I said, and picked up the pen to continue with the file.

~

'I'm going soon,' another lady told me. 'I know it. I can feel it.'

'Where?'

'My other body, my soul body, it will leave this one,' she patted her chest, 'and it will become light. And my light, it will go to the palace where we all go, and my light will become part of the great palace at the centre of everything. There is no day of judgement, we don't come back from the dead, but we go to the palace and become light. I'm going soon.'

She smiled and looked at me with eyes so tired, it was like I could almost see the circuits closing down. I thought of the old relaxation technique that never worked for me. They tried teaching it to us in school as a way to meditate in the run-up to our exams. Imagine your toes relaxing, feel them still and comfortable, and your fingertips, let them hang still and calm. You work your way through your body piece by piece, relaxing each part, shutting it down for a rest.

She died a few days later. Her family said she just fell asleep.

~

'I'm not well at the moment. I'm slowly switching off, like a battery,' said a man with hands that had built things, held tools and bricks.

~

'I just want to stop breathing. Can you help me?' A man in a nursing home. I honestly don't know if he was asking me to look after him after death or stop his breathing for him there and then.

~

'Dad survived the Nazis, many wives, and had lots of children and lots of grandchildren. Do you know his mantra?'

'Tell me?'

'Life is for living – and loving.'

~

'Why have you arranged this funeral, darling?' asked the wife.

'Because I don't want you to worry when the time comes,' he replied. 'It's all taken care of.'

She read over the plan and tutted and waved it away. 'A church, flowers. You don't want all of this. You want jazz – and you told me you wanted strippers.'

The old man laughed from lungs over a hundred years old.

'Honestly, I can try to arrange that if you would like,' I said.

His wife looked at me. 'Really?'

'Well – not in the church. But yes, I'm sure I could arrange a jazz band and strippers. If that is what you would like.'

She smiled at her husband. 'See? You should talk to me before you do these things.'

He blinked at her and smiled back. 'Eh, you're too young to be so serious.'

Before I left, he told me, 'Sickness cannot thrive in a whisky-rich environment.'

~

'There's two words that should not exist: *hate* and *bored*. Nothing in life excuses the use of either one.'

The deceased's family relayed this quote of hers to those of us gathered at her graveside.

'And then,' said her daughter, 'she told me to make my bed as soon as I got up every morning. She said it's like leaving yourself a gift come bedtime.'

I've been trying to make the bed as soon as I get up ever since.

~

I was sitting on a small stool beside a couple in their bed. One of them was passing away, the other waiting, watching. Hoping that somehow the pendulum might swing back the other way. Back to life, to the past years before the end was in sight. Planning the funeral together seemed to bring them some peace.

A huge dog padded into the room and jumped up onto the bed with them, manoeuvring itself awkwardly until it lay on the pillow, its nose near the face of the person for whom we were planning the funeral.

'Is there anything you need?' the partner said.

'Just for you to stay with me,' the dying person replied.

I finished writing my notes and stood up to leave. The dog and the person on the bed looked up at me with the same rheumy eyes. The partner walked me to the door.

'Thank you for coming to see us,' they said.

'Look after yourself. When you need us, you know where we are.'

They smiled and looked back at the bedroom down the hallway.

'How soon do I have to call you?'

'Well, we won't come until you call, so if you haven't called, then we aren't on the way.'

They stood quietly, time slipping out the front door, through the windows, rushing away down the street, unstoppable.

'Take care,' I said.

They nodded, smiled through the exhaustion. 'It's so peaceful,' they said, and closed the door behind me.

~

'It's been a good life. It doesn't matter what comes after. If there is more, then let's have at it, but if this is all there is, then this is more than enough. It's been good.'

~

'I feel like I'm using up someone else's time, like I've been here long enough and I'm stealing days from someone else's account. I should go now.'

~

'You know, she hung on until she was ready.'

'That sounds good.'

'She wanted to see Trump out, but she didn't want to stick around long enough for a telegram from Charles. Now, if it had been the Queen, she might have hung on but.'

~

'Is Dad really dead?' a woman asked down the phone.

'He is, I'm sorry to say.'

'Could you check? I mean, I know he is, and I understand, but could you check? He asked for me to double-check. He didn't trust doctors. Could you check?'

'I'll call you back in a few minutes.'

I called the mortuary and asked if they wouldn't mind checking. 'I know, but she's asking it. It clearly means a lot to her, so if you could just check ...'

Our mortuary attendant came back on the line a few moments later. 'Definitely dead,' she said.

I called the daughter back. 'He's definitely gone,' I told her.

She sighed. I knew she'd done it for her dad. But I also knew, however ridiculous it may have been, that she'd clung to another five minutes of hope.

Books

At around age thirteen, books became one of the most important things in my world. Before then, I'd frowned my way through Alistair MacLean novels and struggled with Biggles, but as hormones and girls appeared, I discovered books.

I had a battered paperback copy of *Christine* by Stephen King, easily the longest book I had ever held, and I wasn't allowed to read it. My mother had deemed it too horrific, likely filled with brutality and sex and chaos. She'd not read it, but King's reputation preceded him.

I'm likely the only male in history who locked himself in the bathroom to read a book at age thirteen. Once my bookmark got to the midway point, Mum gave up her protests, and I spent every evening scrambling through the book. On finishing it, I read more, then more, to the point that these days if I don't have a book in my bag with me, I feel incomplete. At times when depression has washed over the bows of my world, Mel has noticed it's because I'm not reading. She sees there isn't a book on the bedside table, and soon after that my mood dips.

Books, I find, are essential in life and remain so after death. If at a funeral I hear, 'Oh, his favourite book was *East of Eden,*' then I'll read *East of Eden*, looking for insights into the person.

Books are beautiful boxes of magic, and bookshops the most peaceful places on earth.

~

I pulled the hearse up outside the house and walked to the door. The wife of the deceased met me there and smiled weakly.

'Are you ready?' I asked.

She shook her head. 'I don't think I ever could be.'

I had asked her if she wanted to come along when I delivered her husband to the crematorium.

'Is that normal?'

'There's no normal anymore. If it would make things easier for you, I can pick you up early, say around 9am, and we'll take a gentle trip to the crematorium, and you can say a few words over his coffin.'

She looked uncertain, but then nodded. 'I can do that?'

'Yes.'

'You've done it before?'

'I have, a few times. Only when it feels like it might help.'

She nodded. 'I think it would. Help, I mean.'

I walked her to the hearse and held the door for her. The back of the hearse was blacked out with covers so no one could see the coffin. She settled in the passenger seat, and I started the engine, moving slowly away from the kerb. She was silent for the first few minutes and that was fine – sometimes my passengers don't talk, sometimes they talk nonstop.

'I still can't get used to him being gone.'

He'd been ill a long time. She'd nursed him at home until the end. The relationship had shifted from things done together to things done for him, food brought to his bed, medications administered, crosswords done at his bedside – and then done alone when he stopped answering the clues read aloud.

'I know. You'll still be reaching for two mugs when you make tea for a long time yet, I'd imagine.'

She watched the road as we drove. I pointed out the school where my wife works.

'She's a teacher?'

'Yes. A teacher married to a funeral director. We look after both ends of life, and we meet each January when she's not marking and I'm off work. Each year I'm a little greyer and a little wider.'

She was quiet, so I carried on. 'Then we read books, ignore the kids, eat salmon and drink gin and tonic. It's good.'

'I haven't read a book in a long time,' she said. 'I used to read a lot, but these last few years there's not been time.'

We passed into the Sydney Harbour Tunnel.

'There's always another book to read,' I said as we nudged along.

Other drivers always do a slight double take when they realise it is a hearse beside them. A hearse means a coffin, and a coffin means a body. I was driving past a building site once when we had to stop at a red light. Several of the older tradesmen turned and, on seeing us, doffed their hard hats and bowed their heads. It was a brief and simple moment, but also one that was appreciated. I saw it, my colleague saw it and I hope the family in the cars behind us saw it. Two seconds later, the lights turned green, and we moved onward.

'What should I read?' she asked me.

We moved back into daylight and the morning traffic. 'Everything. I've just finished a crazy book called *Lanny* by Max Porter.'

'How was that?'

'Strange, beautiful, very brief.'

She thought about it and then said, 'I think I want a classic. I don't think I am ready for anything new.'

'Then *Don Quixote* is your man.'

She smiled. 'You've read *Quixote*?'

'I think it would be impossible to do this job without having read it.'

She told me about reading it years before. Then talked to me about Dickens and Tolstoy, and we both agreed on *Wuthering Heights* being a great book about mad buggers.

We arrived at the crematorium, and I reversed into the delivery area at the back. The men there nodded at us and introduced themselves to the widow. We slid the coffin out, and she said a brief prayer over it, touching her husband's nameplate. Then, gently, we slid him onto the trolley, and the men wheeled him away. She watched and thanked them, and we climbed back into the hearse.

She was quiet again as we drove past the trees and gravestones and then out into traffic and back towards the constantly busy world.

'Thank you,' she said.

I said it was no problem at all.

'I'm going to read a book soon, I think,' she said.

'Well, if you're ever stuck for a recommendation, give me a call.'

~

Another widow called about her husband's death certificate a few weeks after the funeral. She asked how I'd been, and I said I'd been forcing myself to read of late, as I was working too much and not taking time to be still.

'What are you reading?'

'*The Pillars of the Earth.*'

'Ken Follett?'

I said yes.

'That's older than Methuselah,' she said with a laugh. 'Actually,' she said, 'I'm reading his latest one. Another brick of a book.'

Her husband had bought it, she said, several weeks ago. He'd hefted it as he arrived home and sighed before saying, 'You know, love, I don't think I have the time left for this one.'

I've always said there is time for another book. That was the first time I realised that there comes a point where there isn't time. An eight-hundred-page doorstop of a novel and the time it demands can become more than the days you feel you have left.

'Is it good?' I asked her.

'Oh God, no,' she said, laughing, 'but he would have loved it.'

~

She'd never travelled, we were told. In a room full of books, floor to ceiling, our trolley now held a deceased woman. The hallway was lined with books. I was scanning the shelves: everything from Dickens to Dostoyevsky, Sidney Sheldon to Margaret Atwood.

There was a book with a page earmarked on the coffee table. The last one she had been reading – a non-fiction book about early ocean exploration.

'She always had a book,' we were told. Should she keep her last one, we asked.

'Yes'.

We slipped it into her hands, and took her away.

~

Our funeral home had a space that we needed to fill, a building entrance that we didn't use that had become a vacant recess, often filled with coffee cups and chocolate wrappers. We tried placing a pot plant there, but one weekend it opted to go home with a patron from a local pub, a trail of dirt and dismay scattered along the street.

The space kept collecting litter, coffee cups, tissues, face masks and cigarette butts, so I asked if we could install a street library, have something custom-made to fill the space. I thought it would be shot down, but approval was given and measurements taken, and a carpenter nodded and said he'd be back to us within a few weeks.

Then, to my joy, a beautiful black cabinet was installed, multiple shelves inside. I filled it one Saturday with books from home that I had read and clicked it shut. As I walked back to the car, I heard it click open and felt such a rush of happiness. I love all street libraries, and I adore my one. It's technically the funeral home's library, but I think everyone here knows it is mine, really.

Every Monday after the weekend, I rustle through its shelves, culling the occasional *Real Estate Handbook* or *Accounting for Dummies*, or one too many Lee Child novels. I rearrange the books in height order, theme order, whatever order feels good for that day, and the world feels right to me. During the day, we hear the door click open and closed, books coming and going, stories finding new homes, and the muffle of conversation as people stop their day for a few minutes and recommend books to each other.

There was a suggestion that we place some leaflets in there with guidance for 'What to Do When Someone Dies', but I've held off on that. It's a cabinet of adventure, horror, thrills and life. It's there if you have time in your day or week for a chair, a cup of tea and a good read.

It's there for if there's still the time for another book.

Covid

Covid made our job far simpler, though it broke so many hearts. All of our funerals where 400 attendees were expected became ten-person-only funerals or, at times, two-person-only. We had to observe mandatory mask-wearing, and then there were the periods when we had to check for vaccinations on phone apps. This made the entry to churches far slower and caused huge confusion among some of our older attendees, who were torn between terror of Covid, disbelief in Covid, a need to grieve lost friends at a ceremony, and a pressing desire to hide away at home.

Then, at some services, there would be at least one attendee who would loudly proclaim that Covid was a myth, that none of this was necessary, that they'd read the science and knew masks did nothing and that they refused to wear one. Gently, but firmly, we would then have to deny them entry. Sometimes they'd pop a mask on only to remove it during the service, and we'd have to ask them to put it back on or leave. There'd be tension, disagreement, but we always had the complete backing of the clergy, who, presented with multiple funerals per week, needed as much protection as possible from potential infection. Usually, people would capitulate, but sometimes we'd have dramatic exits – and it would, of course, be our fault. We would take the heat, the abrupt – and on occasion abusive – commentary, the gestures and the aggression.

Covid was bunk, we should know better.

We were told this many times. It was all made up, all a fraud, all an effort to control the population, man. Having seen inside nursing homes, where complete lockdown was in effect, I was leaning more towards science than conspiracy. Covid was serious. Covid was here. We all needed to do whatever was asked of us.

I caught the (hopefully) last of the Delta variant in 2021 and almost missed Christmas with my family. I know how brutally it can knock you down. I don't think I have ever felt as ill as I did those two weeks. Triple-vaccinated as I was, I was still completely floored. Mel and the kids moved out to a friend's home, and I was left coughing incessantly with no sense of smell (which I still only partially have back). During this time, a journalist friend took my photo through my bedroom window for a piece in the *Sydney Morning Herald*. I spent two weeks at home, called most days by the hospital, logging my oxygen saturation statistics, watching some of the worst television ever made and replying to texts from neighbours. (*Haven't heard you coughing – if you don't write back, I'm calling an ambulance.*)

Orange juice and food was dropped on my doorstep, and I came away feeling incredibly lucky – lucky to have a group of friends who helped, lucky not to have been hospitalised, lucky to have got over it, and lucky to have been forced to stop, sit and be simply thankful for the people who were contacting me in whatever way they could. Even now, over a year later, I still can't smell roasting lamb, apple pie, butterscotch and, most bizarrely of all, my son. My wife assures me his room stinks of typical teenage boy, but for me there's nothing there.

The other side-effect of Covid for me was that during my illness I started watching nonsense on Netflix and stumbled onto a show called *Chicago Fire*. Beautiful firefighters putting out beautiful fires. In my moderate delirium, I realised I was fascinated by one of the firemen, finding him oddly beautiful to look at. I told my wife about this: *I'm home feeling awful and finding a TV fireman to be astonishingly attractive.* I knew Covid could take away your sense of smell and stamina, but it was seemingly turning me towards the opposite gender as well. Mel found it amusing, and now, when I still watch the same daft show (I'm thirteen seasons in), she and the kids ask me over and over who my pretty fireman is.

I still think he's pretty.

~

Just before Covid reared its head and turned the street outside our office into a deserted Wild West town – one where I saw a jogger at 6.30am one morning running by in the middle of the road with no traffic coming in either direction – an email came in through our website asking for help in the pre-planning of a husband's funeral. I read it, and replied with a little information, and shortly afterwards I was talking with a lady called Jude who was on the slow road towards her husband's death. The initial plan was hundreds of people and a casket, and a flag on the casket. By email and phone, we worked things through – sometimes stopping as her husband awoke in the background – until we got to the point where, when he passed, we would be ready.

As his health worsened, the scale of the pandemic did as well. Funeral number restrictions started to come in, along with semi-regular and confusing updates that left us scrambling to assimilate the latest changes. As I say, at the worst point it was two people only, in churches that could seat hundreds.

Families would arrive when numbers were limited to ten and there would be twelve of them. *Surely the children don't count as a person?* I'm afraid it's not the age, it's the lungs. *Come on, you're being ridiculous.* It's not me, it's the ruling passed down. *But we've driven from Woop Woop.* I'm sorry, some of you can watch from outside on your phones. Then came the tempers, the tears, the fact that one of the worst days was now worse still.

Exemptions were applied for, rules breached, and arguments had. Nursing homes could hardly have people in to visit. Picking up a deceased lady one morning, I saw a son shouting through a pane of glass to his father in what had become a surreal version of visiting time. The father was confused, losing focus, and the son on the other side of the glass so clearly wanted to hold his dad, to be at his dad's side. Standing there in a mask and gloves, I felt utterly criminal, being inside collecting the dead while the living couldn't hold their family's hands, kiss cheeks, present them with new grandchildren and great-grandchildren.

We were locked at ten attendees when Jude called me to say her husband was on his way out.

'Ten,' she said.

I said I was afraid so.

She gave a long pause, and then said, 'Well, okay. Ten there in the chapel, and four hundred watching on the livestream. Everything else as we planned.'

And it was. We had the casket she had chosen – not a coffin, but a full casket. We had the flag and flowers. We had beautifully stoic Jude and her stepdaughter, her husband's first wife and several military colleagues from the army. One gentleman outside at some distance was snapping photos with his long lens through the door of the chapel. The eulogies were given, the slideshow played. The room, with its distanced seating, looked like something from before the Berlin Wall fell. But behind us, through the lens of the video camera, were four hundred more people, watching and caring and loving. Jude knew they were there, silent as they were, and things happened as we had always planned.

After the funeral, I took her husband's ashes home to her, and we chatted, and life ticked on around the world. Then Jude called me a few months later and wanted to arrange her own cremation. I visited her one afternoon, and we worked through the file and chatted and set the world to rights. When I came back with the contracts for her to sign, she gave me a bottle of purple wine that she had bought from an independent Australian vineyard that was on hard times.

'Now, it's not great wine,' she said, 'but it's good to support small businesses.'

Honestly, my palette is not great, but it was both wine and purple, so I loved it.

~

We never stopped during Covid. Although we were never listed as an essential service, we were constantly working. Funeral sizes shrunk down to two people or ten people, churches were ringing with silence and cemeteries were distanced, with mourners almost hiding behind gravestones and masks.

My family were in lockdown at home, my wife webcasting her classes. (Unfortunately, she was sitting in front of a bookcase full of wine that she'd bought when lockdown was announced, leading to the kids saying, 'Miss, you drink a LOT.') My kids were trying to distance-learn in their rooms, which was the equivalent of suddenly having a day job. Tumble out of bed, down a bowl of porridge, gulp down tea and then log into class. My son, especially, found it hard, and we saw him swing into a mild depression as time away from friends and the isolation settled in.

For myself, sitting at work looking out at the street and quite literally one day seeing a tree branch skitter along the road like a tumbleweed, it was strangely lovely. We distanced at work as much as we could. Washed hands. Wore masks. Echoed through churches surrounded by empty seats. Then I'd come home and see my family emerge like Morlocks from their rooms, blinking at the wide world.

My son's school year missed out on work experience. A while later, after Covid cleared and vaccines settled and we all peeked over the hedgerows and got used to crowds again, Sandy asked if he could do a few days' work with me. Work didn't mind, as long as we kept him away from the mortuary, and we had a suit that fitted him like a glove. So we replaced my six-foot-three lovely boy with a black-suited funeral director – well, until he grinned, and Snapchatted a picture of himself.

I said to work that there'd be no need to pay him, I just wanted him to get a sense of what work was: nine to five, things to be done, time management, life outside of school and so on.

My boss shook her head and said, 'No, we'll pay him.'

For a few weeks he came in, during the school summer break. He learnt to trim coffins; he learnt to wash the car; he worked at our back-of-house, out of my sight; he arrived at funerals in a sharp suit and knotted tie and shiny shoes and stood where I said to stand and did what I asked him to do. I'd say to families ahead of time that my son was working with us for a while, having missed work experience, and asked if they would mind a seventeen-year-old bearer at the funeral. None objected, and Sandy stood outside churches and crematoria chapels handing out orders of service respectfully. I was nervous about having him helping in the cemetery at burials, but he assured me he would be okay. There is something about looking down into a grave as the coffin lowers that is utterly humbling, and very final. The first time he assisted, moving the strap carefully through his hands until the coffin settled on the earth, I wore him out with asking if he was okay.

'It's a big thing, mate. If it's not for you, let me know.'

He smiled and said he was fine, then told me he would be better, though, if he could have a Coke and a cheeseburger. As we drove home from the cemetery, he flicked on an AC/DC song, the sky shone blue and beautiful, and I had a big burst of pride in my chest.

At the end of the first week, we submitted his time sheet, and his pay dropped in and a grin spread across his face. I did mention rent and groceries and paying his way, but we let him spend it on his girlfriend instead.

The thing about raising a happy little atheist was that he found each church I took him into fascinating. The cavernous size of the buildings, the creak and candlelight and echo. I'd give him the backstage tour of each venue and he'd smile wider and tell Mum later about exploring this, that or the other church and meeting a rabbi or a priest or a celebrant.

I left him alone to run errands with Lee one day, and they went on a roundabout drive delivering things, with Lee pointing out various alleyways and houses where he'd had relations as a younger man. Man chat. Man stories. Sandy relayed this over dinner with complete joy – 'Lee had sex with a chick in an alleyway,' which my wife misheard as 'Lee had sex with a chicken'.

Work experience!

Sandy is still on our books. He works with us during school breaks, and once he finishes his HSC, he'll be with us again for a few months before whatever currents catch him and fly him onwards.

I love having him there at the church, introducing him to the priests as 'my son'. Cruising in the car with him on the way to or from a service, talking nonsense and pointing out the huge history of my funeral life, a burial here, a church there; that hospital is where I did this, over there is where I did that.

It's a good thing having kids. I remember bringing him to work once, years before his work experience, on a Saturday when I had a few chores to do. He came along because he knew we had chocolates in the chapel. As I gave him the tour, he stepped up to the lectern in the chapel and tapped the microphone. Around us the sound of his taps resonated from the speakers, and he cleared his throat and then launched into an Eminem song in his pre-puberty squeak of a voice.

Grinning, and very pleased with himself, he rapped the whole of something wildly inappropriate in the funeral home while I sat and clapped along.

~

It was a long day in lockdown. The family were to meet us at the cemetery. The hearse was ahead, and Lee and I were following, enjoying the blue sky and the radio.

I'd needed a fourth bearer for the burial and, after exhausting my options, I had asked if my sister-in-law could assist.

'Can she lift?' my boss had asked.

'She's stronger than me.'

'Does she have smart clothes?'

'I think she'll manage.'

'Okay, then.'

Happily, then, in the midst of the Covid lockdowns, I was able to catch up with Kristal – even if just for a few hours, and in a cemetery.

We arrived, Kristal pulled in a few moments later, and many months of missed hugs ensued, along with texts to both of us from my wife expressing great frustration that she couldn't see her own sister but somehow I was managing it through work. After enjoying catching up, I walked Kristal through things, and then pointed over to the right, where our grave for the day stood, open and waiting.

Kristal did as everyone does the first time they see a grave; she looked over the edge and stared into the depths. Open graves are hypnotic. Then, carefully, she helped us carry the coffin over and settle it onto the bearer bars.

'Now what?' she asked.

'Now we wait for the family,' I said.

A short while later, the family started arriving, and I went over to say hello. They spilled out of their cars, looking relieved that the day was drawing to its end and enjoying the moment of catching up that comes with a funeral.

Then one of them said, 'Why is the coffin over there?'

I looked across. 'I'm sorry, I thought we would settle the coffin in place before you arrived.'

'No, but that is not the grave.'

This is immediately not an argument that you can win. I'd booked the burial with the council; they'd confirmed the grave number that the family owned, and that the previous family member was there. From the council side and the gravedigger's side, this was absolutely the grave.

We walked over, and the family showed me another grave one row up and a few along. The headstone there read with the name of the previous family member who had been confirmed at the other grave. 'This is the grave,' they said.

Deep unease was settling on me, and all I could say was, 'Give me a few minutes.'

I went to the gravediggers, who were there with their backhoe.

'Family says this is the wrong grave. They've shown me another grave just up there with a headstone that matches the name of the person they say is already interred.'

The diggers frowned and pulled out their work orders. The grave they had dug had the deceased in question buried there.

'But we didn't find any trace of a coffin,' one of them said.

Oh.

I tumbled into phone calls. To the council, who started to look into it, saying we could likely bury tomorrow in the other grave; to local funeral homes, to see if someone could house the deceased for a night, should we have to inter the following morning; back to the council, who were still looking into it; back to a funeral home, who gave me a thumbs-up if we needed to deliver the coffin to them and told me they could crew the burial the following day. The council then called me and said they had traced the problem back to an error in their records forty-plus years ago. An incorrect entry that had sat on the file for years, waiting to trip us up at this moment.

The gravediggers said, 'We can dig and bury in the right grave, but it'll take us a few hours.'

I went to the family and, with a deep breath, found them all smiling and seemingly enjoying the day, commenting that Mum loved a bit of drama. I explained the forty-plus-year-old data error that had lain in wait for us, and then explained that we could bury today, but it would take a few hours.

'Then let's play the song, say goodbye, and we will trust you to take care of it,' they said, and all tension left the day. Trust is a wonderful thing.

We played their song, they spoke with love, and then shook our hands and left. And the burial did indeed take place that day.

'Your job is nuts,' my sister-in-law told me after another hug.

Yes. Yes, it is.

I handed her an envelope.

'What's that?'

'Your payment.'

'Seriously?'

'Of course, with thanks from us for the help.'

We hugged again, and then Covid pulled us all back to our extremities and our locked-down lives.

~

We had it easy for the most part. Funeral directors were not locked down, were not forced to work from home. Every day I left Mel and the kids and went to work as normal. They stayed home and fought against the cabin fever and isolation from their friends.

As for the families we spoke to, if they were lucky one of them had been able to see Mum or Dad before they passed. Often it wasn't the case, though. Mum had died without the hand of her daughter on her cheek. Dad had gone with his children not able to be there.

We did our best to be there for those who were dealing with grief in such strange circumstances. A place of calm and respect in the empty streets.

Evening Rosary

A part of a Catholic service can be a rosary the evening before. It is a viewing, but with prayers and memories of the deceased before the grandeur of the service the next day. Typically, it is immediate family, a priest and a funeral director or two quietly at the back of the room.

This night, the coffin was open, and the priest was praying, and I was away from the activity, listening for my cue to return. My colleague was standing at the chapel door, and he gestured me over subtly.

'What is it?'

He nodded out of the door, and I popped my head out into the Bondi evening. Streetlights were on, and the pizza place next door was wafting salami and tomato our way. We had a parking area out the front with neatly trimmed hedges and a bush by the front door. Behind the bush was a hosepipe that we used to wash down the driveway if Saturday night proved too kebab-and-pizza-filled for the drunk folk wandering by us on their way home.

There, by the front door of the funeral home, was a homeless guy. His trousers were off and in a ball on the ground behind him, and he had our hosepipe spraying his testicles and backside, jetting water up between his knees and cheeks, nudging the top of the hose around his skin. The streetlight lit him too well, as did the splash of headlights as they came by. Behind me, I heard the rosary coming to an end and the family thanking the priest.

We knew the homeless would sleep out the front now and then. We had a cover, so there was shelter from the rain. We had bushes, so there was a sense of privacy, I imagine. Of course, the truth is it's not something I can imagine: no matter how erratic life has become I have always had somewhere to sleep, somewhere to brush my teeth and shower. In the mornings, if anyone had slept at the front of the building, they would be gone, and we would sweep and hose off the driveway.

'What do we do?' I asked my colleague. Being still new to funerals, I was prone to panic and trying to solve everything that happened at once.

'Nothing we can do,' he said. His philosophy was that people got the funerals they deserved. If this family deserved, somehow, to come outside and see a homeless man jet-washing his backside clean, then that was what would happen. I hadn't quite grasped that mantra, though over time it has become more and more something I believe. I do realise now that I can't control everything. I can try, but a mistress rushing from the back of a crowd to the graveside is out of my control. A splintered family meeting two separate funeral homes and giving both homes the authority to collect the deceased, causing confusion at the hospital, is out of my control. A piece of music skip-skipping as we try to play it from a scratchy old CD given to us by the family again is sadly out of my control.

What I can control, I keep tightly in my grasp. But when it comes to the hope that the rain will hold off for the burial on Friday, well, my broken foot will still tell me that a storm is coming some of the time.

That night I let the door swing open and loudly said, 'Thank you, Father,' as I turned back to the family. Behind me, I hoped the homeless guy had heard and was finishing up – not moving on to armpits and a full-frontal wash down. The family stopped to look at the fish in our aquarium, they had a chocolate or two from the bowls we had on the tables, they smiled and thanked us for the evening timeslot and sympathised with our families at home having dinner without us. Behind them, the curtains closed on their mother, slowly and silently, ahead of the church service tomorrow. They were smiling at my colleague and me. They were talking about the upcoming funeral. They were moving ever closer to the door and the evening outside and the chap and his exposed backside and deep-cleaning hose.

I stepped back through the door, needing to know before them if they were about to be confronted by a viewing of something that they had not anticipated.

The hosepipe was hanging off the bushes, swinging and dripping down into a large puddle of water. The man was gone. The bushes were damp, as though rain had just stopped.

According to my colleague's funeral code, this family had not deserved to encounter our neighbour's evening wash.

Contemporary Flowers

Once I got used to it, I enjoyed hearse driving. The first few times, it felt like I was manoeuvring some kind of fragile gemstone that could crack or shatter. One of my first days driving was for a funeral in the Garden Chapel behind Sacred Heart Hospice. The hearse was to park under the hospice and reverse into a tiny space to the right of the barrier. Coffin delivered, I commenced the eighty-three-point manoeuvre (which my colleagues could do in three confident swings) to bring the hearse into the bay and, inch by inch, I brought it further into safety. At the last moment, the last metre, the wing mirror clipped on a column, and I put a ten-cent-coin-sized scratch in the paintwork.

One of my colleagues came over and looked at the scratch and nodded, then reminded me, alas too late, that the wing mirrors could fold inwards. My wife had driven us everywhere since we landed in Australia as she 'got car sick' if I drove and, consequently, I had largely forgotten everything I ever knew about cars.

'Dammit,' I said, and my colleague smiled.

~

Hearse driving, I gradually learnt, was almost minimalist. You take as few bends, lane changes and hills as possible to get from A to B. You should never see a hearse crossing lanes on the freeway – it should sit safely in one lane, not too far forward, not too far back, essentially riding the Goldilocks zone of speed and safety. On smaller roads, it shouldn't race to catch the amber light, nor should it lurch from the lights when they turn green. Slow to go and smooth to arrive. If family are following along with you, you drive with one eye on the mirror, watching for the furthest car back. If you lose them at the lights, then you pull over and wait for them to catch up. P-platers will sometimes weave into funeral corteges, not knowing where they are until they see the hearse.

Hearse driving makes you second in command at a funeral. The conductor rides alongside you. If you're in a tight spot, as we were one day in a cemetery where someone had parked a car and then gone for a jog, then you put your faith entirely in the conductor. He stood ahead of me, watching either side of the vehicle, gesturing slightly to his left and to his right while I made minor corrections, moving extremely slowly, watching his hands as he gestured for me to *come on, come on, move to the left, to the left, come on, come on, right*, and then he smiled as we passed the illegally parked car (the jogger was now in the distance, looking embarrassed and afraid) and pulled away from the knee-high wall to the right of the hearse, fitting like thread through a needle.

The conductor jumped back in with me and said, 'Well done,' and we rolled on to the graveside.

Trusting the conductor, I was driving to church one day, coffin in the rear and a floral casket cover on the top. The flowers were sitting on non-slip mats, and we were taking the smoothest, simplest route to the church, when his phone chirped.

'Okay, turn around,' he said and explained that family had decided they wanted to drive with the hearse rather than arrive with it already in place.

'Don't they live ...'

He nodded. Almost forty minutes away.

'They were happy for us to be in place, but this morning ... they've changed their minds.'

He told me to speed up, and we pointed back the way we had come. Behind us, the coffin was safe and the flowers shivering only slightly.

We made good time, careful time, but as we neared the family home, we started to turn onto narrower streets and hills. On the third sharp turn, the flowers behind me tilted and dropped. I swore.

'It's okay. Pull over here,' the conductor said, and I slowed and stopped.

We jumped out, reset the flowers, gathered a few leaves that had come away and placed them back into the arrangement.

Moving forward slowly, turning slowly, we were suddenly cut off by a white SUV that, to this day, I don't think saw the length and breadth of us. I had no choice but to stop abruptly, and the flowers behind us rolled off again.

Again we stopped, and again we repaired and reset, replacing flowers that had come loose and recognising that the neat perfection of the florist's work was now a little more uneven. The colours were still beautiful, the flowers still popped against the dark of the coffin, but there was a sense of artistic chaos creeping in.

We met the family, and they gathered around the hearse, admiring the coffin and commenting on the flowers. How beautifully contemporary they were. How refreshingly original in shape.

Then they moved to their vehicles, and we slowly pulled away. In the rear-view mirror, I saw a white SUV at the back of the cortege line. Perhaps someone else had been running late to meet the family.

The Last Train

'Have you done this before?' I asked my colleague.

He frowned, thought and said, 'Not for a long time. Not for a long time.'

He'd been in the industry for more than forty years.

We were driving through the city to Central Station, nosing the hearse through early-morning taxis and pedestrian crossings and the surge and purge of buses. There is always the moment, at each crossing, where one person will see what we are – a hearse with a visible coffin in the back – and do a double take, which leads to more heads twitching and more eyes seeing, maybe someone making the cross on their chests, other people looking away, and parents rushing their kids to overly expensive city daycare looking upset with us for exposing their child to death.

I've been shouted at outside nursing homes, as we bring someone into care, for not thinking of the children who live in the residential street behind the nursing home. We do things as swiftly and quietly as we can, but sometimes it is midday on a Saturday and kids are playing in the street and we still have to attend. Moments later, a parent rushes out onto the street and makes more of a scene then we ever could. Some people find death offensive. Almost a betrayal. A person alive, a person in nursing care, is normal and acceptable, but a person now passed, now in a body bag and being collected by a funeral home – that shouldn't be. And the men doing it are obviously the worst, somehow brutes or disrespectful.

In fact, sometimes we go to great physical extremes to show respect for the dead. I've carried the deceased down five flights of stairs with a colleague, arms burning, shoulders ready to pop, seeing the vehicle and knowing I have maybe two metres left in me before I am going to drop it. Somehow, we make it; we reach the vehicle and slide the person safely inside. I pull in great lungfuls of air and try to remain composed as the family walk to the vehicle to say goodbye.

I've exited through garage doorways at three in the morning, carefully bringing the person around bicycles and boxes, leaving nothing damaged. Safely lifting, turning, stepping, moving and reaching the vehicle.

One day we collected a lady from the seventh floor of an apartment block. Typically we would use a service elevator, but that day there wasn't one. We had our hand trolley, which has two wheels at the foot end so that we can move people almost as if they are standing. After we had placed the deceased in the body bag, and onto the trolley, the belts cinched tight, we covered the trolley so all was hidden. Then we had the awkward wait for the elevator, hoping it would arrive empty, which fortunately it did.

Inside we pressed Ground, and then had the same discomfort about encountering a neighbour as the elevator dropped, level by level ... and came to a stop on Level Two. The doors opened, and I stepped forward to block the view of the standing trolley as a family of four saw us – parents and their young kids.

'I'm very sorry,' I said, 'but would you mind waiting for the elevator to return?'

The father saw the trolley behind me, then his wife did as well, and I braced myself for a mouthful of abuse, which thankfully didn't come. The father nodded and said, 'No problem.' The mother held the kids to her side and told them to bow their heads, which they did.

'Thank you,' I said, and we dropped to Ground and swiftly left in the wagon.

We are so careful, so slow, so professional, that yes, the occasional bellow of disapproval does rankle. But I understand: for some parents, death is something for their children to know of, but not see – for as long as is possible.

On this day, we nudged through the city, pulled into Central Station, passed the taxi rank and swung around to a large loading roller door. The door slid up, and we backed in. As we began to unload the coffin onto the trolley, a guard came and told us which platform our train was coming in on. Beyond him, the station was vibrant, as Central always is.

Every level of life was there, from the homeless by the entry ways hoping for a dollar or two, to tourists excitedly moving towards today's destination, to city workers cutting through them all like scalpels, knowing exactly where they were going and when they need to be there. Kids in prams were gaping up at the size of things; older kids were hovering by the vending machines on a mission to get Coke and Cheese Twisties for the journey. Pensioners walked through, seeing the station as it would have been decades before, when they were the kids. Everywhere people were on their way, hot coffees and croissants in hand, newspapers under their arms.

Before Central was Central, and such a hub of life, it was the Devonshire Street Cemetery. Many of the newer platforms, all the way across to the Devonshire Street tunnel, are built on top of land that was a graveyard. When the station was built, the bodies were exhumed and reinterred at Rookwood General Cemetery and other locations. In the name of progress, even the permanence of a grave can be disturbed. Once upon a time the dead were brought here on a daily basis, and over five thousand bodies were interred. Now, though, a body at Central is unusual. But today was an unusual day.

Our platform was a way off; we would have to walk up Platform 1 and then turn, heading through the main concourse and along. The guard spoke on his radio and kept us with him for a moment, and then said 'okay' as he received word that our train had pulled in. Ideally, we didn't want to be exposed to the crowds for too long.

We began to wheel the trolley with the coffin on top through the station towards the platform. My colleague walked at the foot, which always leads, and I had my hands either side of the head. Walk slowly, don't make eye contact, dignified and steady. Within a few steps, people started seeing what we were doing, by the time we reached the concourse, there was a ripple developing around us. Passengers were reacting nervously or simply staring. There were no two ways about it, there was a dead body on the platform, albeit within a coffin.

We reached the platform; the train was there. Halfway down, a guard was waiting for us. He showed us inside the train and we looked in at the close space we had to deliver the coffin into. It would travel by train through the countryside and be retrieved, far down the line, by another funeral home.

'Tight,' my colleague said, looking at the corners between the doors, the entry passage and the holding shelf.

'Yup,' the guard replied.

No matter the weight, somehow, we always lift and always manage. The bad back comes a day or so later, when I'm doing little more than picking up a sandwich or laundry basket. That day, I lifted the head as my colleague lifted the foot, and we moved a metre from the trolley into the train and placed the foot of the coffin on the shelf. My colleague then gave guiding directions as I gently pushed the coffin home, trying not to groan, gasp or grunt. Once we had gently wrestled the coffin in, the guard secured it in place. Then we stepped back, pausing to bow before walking away.

I collapsed the trolley and carried it at my hip. On the walk back, we drew far less attention, now being merely two overdressed men, one of whom was awkwardly carrying a silver contraption at his hip.

Behind us, the train shunted out of the platform and carried the deceased away. The clock ticked over to 8.30, and we drove back to base to load the vehicle again and head to church, back on far more familiar ground.

I've always thought it would make a great start to a gothic novel: an early-morning train receiving a coffin on board, delivered by a dusty old funeral home. The train leaving, people settling for their long journey, and the coffin there in its place, shrouded in mystery, waiting for a delay and a dark tunnel for the chills and thrills to begin. Maybe it's more suited to a Victorian-era novel. A Dracula situation.

It felt truly old-school, though, to be walking the coffin along the train platform that early, sending pigeons up in swirls as we brought the deceased to the platform on time, and sent them on their way on their last train, at a station built on an old cemetery.

The Date and the Time

Funerals are announced in the newspapers, and we as funeral directors labour over the details that go into the notice: the names, the grandchildren's names, the sons-in-law and daughters-in-law and, importantly, the location and time of the service. Families also often let social media spread the word of the when and where. Text messages float like seeds on the wind, passing from phone to phone as they give the details.

Life is busy, though, and sometimes the details blur and people arrive rushing and breathless only to find that it's not the day, and it's not the time.

~

We were at a favourite church of mine, like a little slice of England on a summer's day. The hearse shone by the front door. Outside, the main road buzzed past us and we could hear the sound of ever-present building works just up the road, just down the road, and even from within the church itself. The coffin had been taken inside after we called the clergy. Since then, we had been taking names in the memorial book and handing out orders of service, bottles of water and packets of tissues. The tissues baffle people. I think they must expect them to be chocolate, because they pick up them up, then startle at the softness of the package and then say, 'Oh! Oh, I imagine this makes sense.'

The last few arrivals were running up the gravel driveway and we were waving to them to slow down and take their time.

'It's okay, it's only just started. Don't risk an ankle, you're okay.'

High heels on gravel driveways can lead to mishap.

They quickly scribbled down their names, took some tissues, and then we murmured to them about silencing their mobile phones. Everyone else in the church had been reminded to silence their phones at the start of the service, so it was only latecomers who ran the risk of being That Person.

So, we reminded the latecomers to *please silence your phone as you step inside*, and then we started to dismantle our table. At this point in a funeral, we have roughly forty-five minutes to clean down, pack away, keep an eye on things inside the church (any coughing should be met with a water bottle delivered to the person, any parents struggling with a pram should be assisted, any concerned glances from the clergy should be met with a response). Sometimes, something is missed – a reading, a slideshow – and we monitor what is happening inside, fingers moving down the page. Yes, the nephew reads the verse; yes, the hymns are sung; yes, the eulogies are complete; but, no, the slideshow has been skipped. We've jumped to a hymn further down. At this point I write *SLIDESHOW* in a message on my phone and walk to the lectern, lean in to the minister and hold the screen up to his eyeline and he glances, nods, mouths *Thank you* and, after the hymn ends, he stands and asks the congregation to please turn and look at the screen and some beautiful memories.

On this day we were observing our usual duties, when two people approached and asked about the funeral inside. I told them the name of the deceased and invited them in, but they shook their heads. I had given them the wrong name. They asked about the next funeral, and I said we were the only one in the church that day. They looked concerned, and I asked for the name of the service they were expecting and called the church office. I recited the name and was told what I was expecting to hear, the service they were attending had been held the day before.

'I'm sorry, that service was yesterday.'

They started chastising themselves. Tears welling in their eyes.

'It's okay, there's nothing can be done about it now. Perhaps if the service yesterday was live-streamed you can still view the link?'

There had been an email, there had been a link.

Taking in their distress, I suggested something unusual. 'Then look, it's not normal but how about, if you have earphones, you find a quiet corner in the church and watch the service?' I directed them to a few chairs upstairs and away from the crowd. 'Be discreet and you can time-travel, sit today and watch yesterday.'

~

At a crematorium, with a service just beginning, a couple approached me. I told them the name of the service inside the chapel, and they stopped. It wasn't the name they were expecting. They told me they had been told absolutely this chapel, and absolutely this time.

I checked the crematorium website and agreed with them, this chapel, this time, but next week.

'You're a week early, I'm afraid.'

They stared dumbfounded, and then started to laugh.

'It's good to rehearse things,' I said, and then directed them to the cafe. 'You may as well get a coffee and a cake while you're here, and I hope all goes well next week.'

They walked away laughing, which made a nice change from how we usually see people leaving a funeral.

~

She rushed up the stairs, eyes red and raw and her coat half on and half off.

'It's okay,' I said to her, stepping forward to take the coat.

'I can't believe I'm late. To my own mother's funeral.'

I shook my head. 'You aren't late.'

She looked at her watch and shook her head. 'I really am.'

'You're perfectly on time.'

Coat off, she was looking through the doors beyond at her mother's coffin and the gathered attendees. There was a picture on the screen of her mother smiling. She looked at her watch again.

'Don't worry. Nothing starts until I say it starts, and nothing would have started without you being here. And now you are here, so if you are ready, we'll walk inside and we'll begin. Exactly on time.'

She smiled. 'So, I'm not late?'

'Not at all.'

She stepped to the door, and I nodded for the concierge to start the first piece of music. The celebrant stood and smiled from the lectern, reaching out her arms in welcome to the daughter, who walked to her seat at the front of the chapel, perfectly on time.

The Box

At the coroners, instead of a body bag, we were brought a cardboard archive box, of the kind you would see in an office holding old records. The box was placed on the trolley, and we signed the ledgers. The coroner looked at the cardboard box as we picked it up and there was a crackle of unspoken fury. A human life reduced to just a cardboard box – the only remains that had been found of her so many years later.

We said our thankyous and, rather than place the box in the back of the wagon, we drove with it on my lap. A few streets down the way, my colleague said, 'It's not right.'

'I know what you mean.'

The box was too light in my hands. 'You know what I'd prefer?' I asked.

He shook his head.

'I'd rather we just drove her all the way, not to our mortuary. Too many people have been involved, all with the best intentions, but I'd rather we just drove her home – that we were the last people to carry her before she's home.'

He nodded and, for a moment, the thought hung in the air. It would be a long drive, and we'd cop a lot of grief for it, but the idea of passing her along to another set of hands felt wrong.

We stopped at the lights and my colleague looked at the box.

'I know what you mean,' he said, as the lights hung red.

We could just drive. Quietly, safely, directly. Take her all the way home.

The lights went green, and we knew we couldn't. We knew the next team was ready for her, and the next hands on the box would be respectful and careful, and the hands at the other end would be similarly caring, and then the final hands at the final destination would bring her into care, and she would be home. We were a link in the chain, a chain that should never have been needed but for one man's brutality.

Deaths by domestic violence, and the bodies that come to us broken and beaten and defiled by men, stop our world and make us sick. I've seen cases with defensive wounds on their hands as they've raised them to try to stop the attack. I was told once that children don't have such wounds as they don't expect the violence. The things that men do and the toxic violence under their skin, the evidence of which was here in the box I was holding – I hate it. Sitting with the box in my lap, I hated that this woman was no longer free to live, to be, to make mistakes and be herself, all because one man had taken it into his head to destroy her.

We placed her in our mortuary, and my colleague parked the car. The following day, we handed her on to the next crew, who would take her closer to home. Home to whatever peace lay at the end of such a road.

~

The things we see stay with us; they stay with me. We all know we are going to die; we live with that and consign it to the backs of our minds until we are forced to bring it forward. But death should come at the end of a long life, lived fully and loved.

I told my children about the box. I honestly think that the best thing we can do to counter domestic violence is raise better children. Children who will grow into adults who won't bully. Who won't beat. Who won't kill their partners.

Raise better children.

Make these chains of caring, careful hands a thing of the past.

The Urn

I had a family wanting a church and three limousines, hundreds of dollars' worth of flowers, and an opera singer. A family with money to spend that could create a purity for their deceased. The list of requirements was ever-growing and pulling all of my attention.

I also had one chap, at home on his own, with only his television.

He had placed a cup of tea in front of me when we met. He'd made one for himself, and I saw a third sitting on the counter in the patch of sunlight from the window. As we talked, I found myself thinking about the opera singer. He told me about his wife, and I was trying to quash thoughts about newspaper notices for another service. He told me about his wife with affection, about lost siblings and friends and the feeling that he was now the last one standing.

'You'll bring me the ashes?'

For a moment I thought he was speaking over the phone, and I stared at my hand, dumbly looking for the handset. Then I shivered and focused on him as I replied.

This wasn't my best day. It's a long time ago now, and it's a day I feel I have learnt from. Nothing is as important as the person right in front of you or speaking to you on the phone. Everything else is noise. Focus on the person you are with, and everything else can and must wait.

'In a day or so, yes.' A no-service cremation.

'I'd like an urn. A simple box.' He handed me a picture. I knew our catalogue had something similar. His voice was barely a whisper.

'That will be no trouble at all.'

The sunlight from the window was pooling and spilling down the formica of the countertop. In my head, the countdown was ticking towards the time when I would need to have locked in my newspaper notices, located a priest and clarified the cost of the singer.

These were early days, when I had just started with church funerals instead of smaller services. When I was trying to overthink everything and rush ahead.

~

A few days later there were four phone messages in one hour. All from him, all asking about his wife's ashes.

I looked at the shelf behind me, and they were there. The urn had come in as well; it was on my desk, and I chastised myself for not having seen it.

I confirmed she was here with me.

'Can you bring her home today?'

I looked at the paperwork in front of me and realised that it would be done. I *would* complete these things if I just stopped trying to do everything at once – if I stopped and focused on things one at a time. Piece by piece. I had to build the jigsaw sequentially, rather than trying to start in the middle and work my way out.

'Please?'

The most important piece was returning his wife to him.

'I'll come now,' I said. I transferred the ashes to the urn.

~

He took her from me and moved through the house quickly. A small lounge with a muted television playing, beyond which I could see the single bedroom. All the curtains were drawn, and the air was heavy with coffee and candle wax.

He went into the bedroom, placed her on the far pillow and lay down on the bed. He looked to me and waved me away. I turned, feeling suddenly that I was present at a moment of intimacy that I should not intrude upon.

'My love,' I heard him say.

I saw a photograph of her in her twenties in the lounge as I left, holding a puppy that was gnawing at one of her hands. She was staring straight at the camera and the future, smiling. Shouting from the past, 'I'm going to do something; I'm going to be something!'

I heard him clear his throat and say from the bedroom behind me, 'Thank you for bringing her home.'

I called that it was no worries and wished him well. I clicked the door closed behind me.

A plane cut the sky above, punching through the clouds and disappearing. A garbage truck lumbered past, spilling empties from a recycle bin. A school playground thronged with catcalls and demands for cigarettes. A man yelled into his phone, walking on the street ahead of me, shouting bitter expletives. A dog strained at a chain a few houses up, spittle flying from its teeth as it barked.

They fell silent to my ears as a husband used his breath to sing to his wife. Softly, his voice slipping through the open window. She'd been loved. She'd been so very loved. As life took its turns and twists, she had been loved. And now she was missed terribly.

Take care of things as quickly as you can, I learnt that day. A half-hour delay for me could be a lifetime for someone else. There is nothing more important than bringing comfort to someone when they are grieving. The days of lasagnes and casseroles being delivered to the door by friends and neighbours seem to have gone. The offer of walking a person's dog so they could stay home with memories. Or of checking in with a bottle of wine, or two coffees and a cake, just to see if today is the day that the faucet turns and the emotions come rushing out.

The world rushed back in as I settled into the car. Schoolkids surging from the gate, buses grunting to the kerb, the dog barking, snapping large mouthfuls of air and chewing them up. I turned the ignition and pointed myself back towards the office and the work that needed to be done.

Two Funerals and Two Weddings

In 2002 Mel sat on the toilet and asked me to marry her. She said it'd make the visa easier, with us looking to move to Australia. I was in the bath, slowly destroying bubble islands with well-placed flicks of water, in my head a merciless supervillain. It took a moment to register what she had said.

'Did you just propose?'

Mel looked momentarily caught in the headlights, but then said, 'I think I did, yes.'

To be clear, the toilet lid was down, and she was only sitting.

'Well, then, I do,' I said.

'Hold on, if I'm engaged, I need a ring,' she said.

Behind her on the cistern, I saw a green plastic Christmas cracker ring that had been knocking around for a few months. I climbed out of the bath and handed her the ring, and we were suddenly engaged, and she was on the toilet, and I was naked.

'Uhm,' we both said, and immediately decided not to tell any family. This would be a registry office wedding: two witnesses and a damn good curry. No chaos or church bells. Just us in the belly of London, married.

We told our housemate, Neil, and his eyes turned red. He bolted out and bought champagne. Joy is infectious, and almost as intoxicating as champagne, and we celebrated, feeling quite pleased with ourselves and this secret squirrel wedding we were planning. Then, several champagnes down, Mel called her mum in Australia and announced she was engaged, resulting in much mayhem on the Central Coast. Then we carried on drinking.

Mel told me that no way was she taking my name. 'You only change your name for an upgrade, and Gosling is not an upgrade,' she said. There was no Ryan at this time.

~

The following day, Mel's brother called from Sydney. He needed to speak to Mel urgently. Mel took the phone, blinking away the night before, the green plastic ring on the bedside table.

'What have you done?' he asked. 'Mum says you're in trouble.'

Mel sat up and assured him she wasn't in any trouble. 'I'm getting married.'

'Are you sure you're not in trouble?'

I saw her stretching in bed, holding the phone to her ear as I carried a cup of tea through to her.

'Well, I don't *think* so,' she said, looking at me.

~

We tiptoed around, quietly happy with the engagement but not telling anyone beyond, seemingly, the whole of Australia.

Then, a few days later, my mum called and told me my grandfather had died. You may remember him from earlier – the man who believed he was Jesus. He was a fractious man, a difficult man, but he was my grandfather, and I had a lifetime of knowing him and loving him.

Mel hugged me as we both scratched our head, reconciling the troublesome man Mel had met with the ideal of a grandfather. I called my dad to let him know. Though my parents were divorced, it seemed appropriate to tell him his ex-father-in-law had died.

'Well,' he said, 'we never got on but I'm sorry to hear that.'

The following morning, Dad called back.

'Hey,' I said. Two phone calls in two days was a record for any English son and his father.

'Uhm, I'm really sorry, but Grandad died this morning.'

'That's …' I started but couldn't continue.

Both grandfathers, in twenty-four hours.

Mel was looking at me, and I mouthed, 'Grandad died.'

She looked confused and said, 'We know that.'

'No, my other grandad.'

Her hand went to her mouth, and I tried to think of something to say.

'I'll see you soon,' I said, and my dad told me he'd let me know when and where the funeral was to be, which was almost exactly what my mother had said the day before.

'Two grandfathers in two days,' I said and sat down.

'Fuck,' Mel said.

~

A few weeks earlier I had received another call from my dad. He'd told me that Grandad was in a bad way and asked if could I go over and see how things were. My dad was away in Spain on holiday. I packed a quick bag and caught a train and spent a few nights with my younger brother. I went to see Grandad, who was in bed and unconscious. My nan was warm and welcoming, but her gaze was constantly on the bedroom door, where we could hear grandad inhaling and exhaling with long, rumbling breaths. While I was there, the doctor came. After spending some time in the bedroom, he came out and said, 'He's on his way out. With no water and food, he'll likely be gone soon.'

'And with water?' Nan asked.

The doctor looked at his feet and then said, 'With water, it could be several weeks.'

Nan nodded and said, 'Bless,' and, as the doctor left, she went to the kitchen and filled a glass with water and brought it to the bedroom with a teaspoon. She trickled some into Grandad's mouth and set the glass to one side. She touched his forehead and said it again, 'Bless.'

She smiled, and I knew she'd be giving Grandad water every hour or so. Drawing out his end of life with such constant love and ministry. Warm, safe water trickling between his lips a droplet at a time while his wife stroked his forehead and whispered simply, 'Bless'.

He died in bed with her beside him.

~

Funerals suddenly started appearing on the horizon and, like most people my age, I really hadn't been to many. Mum's dad was to be first, then two days later, Dad's dad. Mum's dad, the self-proclaimed Jesus, war hero and opinionated dictator, was to see his way out at a London crematorium. My father's dad, a gentle man plagued with arthritis who'd had an array of medications for most of the time I had known him, dished out daily by Nan, was to have his service at a crematorium in Milton Keynes.

As we travelled to the first funeral, Mel said, 'Maybe we should tell your family – about the wedding?'

I shook my head, still wanting to keep things quiet. Mel had a ring now, a vintage piece we'd picked up at the market. I had a sneaking feeling someone would spot it and figured if they did, we'd deal with that there and then.

Grandad's funeral was led by Uncle Steve – scaffolder, limousine driver, rugby fanatic and six-foot-seven behemoth. Beside him was Aunty Dawn, five-foot-nothing and ever struggling with alcoholism. I'd not seen much of them in the last few years and we said, as I hear at funerals almost every day, 'Oh, it's so wonderful to see you, it's been so long. It's a shame about the circumstances.'

My mum sat sobbing; my aunt as well. Mel was between them holding their hands. I didn't know any of the few folk in the chapel with us or quite how to behave.

He had been a difficult man, the man there in the box. Furiously opinionated and certain of himself. Wilful in his ability to insult. At the same time, though, he had been gifted with rhyming and poetry, though he only ever wrote about Jesus. He'd read lengthy pieces down the phone and, subject matter aside, I could never fault the rhyming structure. The one certain thing we'd had in common was a love of the blank page and the joy of filling it with something that hadn't existed until we willed it to be so.

Uncle Steve stood at the lectern. Years before his oesophageal cancer.

'Dad wanted to be left to science, but science, it seems, didn't fucking want him.' There was a ripple of nervous laughter around the chapel. 'But yesterday I managed to get rid of his brain. I mean, it was donated to this group who ... shit, I don't know, wanted brains. So, they have his brain. And it was a good brain. It was his brain. Sorry I couldn't give more of you away, Pop.'

Steve looked at the coffin behind him, the coffin that, to me at that time, seemed almost ridiculous – clichéd and artificial. Was he even in there?

It wasn't ridiculous to Steve, or Mum or Dawn, though. I could see that. It was their dad, their father-in-law. And to Mel it was a slice of my history, of who and how I am.

Steve cleared his throat and continued. 'Dad was a cantankerous fucker. He always had the last word. Even if I hung up on him, he'd call me a day later to throw the last word on whatever we'd been arguing about. When sis and I were clearing his house, we found a box of condoms, with two missing, some pornography' – my mum flinched at this and shouted, '*Steven!*' and he laughed her away with a wave – 'and a tape marked *My Funeral*. The old bugger recorded his own eulogy. So here he is, having the last word.'

Steve held a small cassette player to the microphone and pressed *Play*. After a short hiss, my grandfather's voice came on. 'If you're listening to this, then I must have passed on. Welcome, my friends, I am so glad you all came to my funeral.'

The sparse population of the room smiled as Cyril led us through his life, his beliefs in Spiritualism, his certainty that he would return and help lead us to better times and his urging that we not be sad.

'After all, I'll see you all soon, over there.' Then he started singing: 'Over there, I'm just over there, I'll see you over there.'

Steve pressed *Stop* and, after a few moments, silence, he looked back at the coffin and said, 'Bye, Pops.' The curtains closed.

In a nearby pub later, Steve walked through to the main bar. We had a room to the back with not many people in it. Grandad had had enough money left in life to lay on some catering, but hardly any of it had been eaten. Steve, being huge, being almost immediately loved by anyone he met, strode into the bar and called for attention.

'Excuse me. My father's funeral was today, and we have all this food and no fucker is eating it. Please come and have a sandwich on Dad.'

The people in the bar looked to the tables where Steve had set sandwiches and sausage rolls and sauce.

'Eat it. Dad hated waste.'

People moved towards the food, thanking him, shaking his hand, looking up at him as he stood just below the ceiling.

As he came back towards us, we saw, at the entry to the room, three elderly men in uniform. Steve walked over to them, and they saluted him. They were from Grandad's regiment and had seen the funeral notice in the paper. They looked to us and saluted again and then they faded away. Maybe not all my grandfather's stories had been embellished.

'Fuck me,' Steve said, sitting down with a thud. 'They said he was a good man. They said he was a good soldier.'

We toasted a good man, a good soldier.

~

Two days later we were lined up outside my paternal grandparents' bungalow in Milton Keynes. As a family we were about to drive to the crematorium. On the way to the bungalow, Mel had again said, 'We should really tell your parents about the wedding.' Again I had said no. The wedding was ours. Split families are a juggle, a stress, and I wanted our day to be our day. It also shouldn't impose on this day – this funeral.

'But you need to tell them we're moving to Australia,' she said.

I nodded. 'Yeah, we'll get to that.'

Nan wouldn't come out. My cousins were there, and my aunts and uncles, and again we were having the odd pleasure of not having seen each other in a long time and finally catching up. I was introducing Mel to everyone while we waited for Nan.

She finally appeared at the front door, and she saw Mel standing by me. She gestured, and Mel walked over. Nan took her arm. She held it tightly as Mel walked her to the car. Nan was shaking, absolutely not wanting this day, this funeral.

Mel came back over, looking shaken. When Nan had first met Mel several months earlier, upon realising they were the same height she had said, 'You're the one,' and kissed Mel on the cheek.

'Thank you,' I said quietly to Mel.

As we walked to the car we were riding in, Mel said, 'We really need to tell them we are getting married.'

I had a feeling Nan had worked it out already. No one commented on the ring, but if anyone knew, Nan did, and if she had worked it out, then she had likely guessed we would be moving to Australia.

'Another day,' we agreed and rolled on to another crematorium.

For my father's father the service was far more traditional. Crematorium chapel, Bible verses, eulogies, favourite music. My dad said years later when I spoke to him about this that he didn't know at the time about civil celebrants, the non-religious alternative for somebody to lead a funeral, or he would have gone that way. They would have had it in a different venue, and with a service more unique and expressive of his dad.

There is nothing at all wrong with a service like the one we had – it had the beats we needed and elicited the grief we needed to release, brought everyone together in one place and put hands on the shoulders they needed to be on, but I remember it far less than I do my other grandad's, despite the fact that I was far closer to my father's father. We were all there for him, and he was in the coffin in the room with us, but it was as though his personality wasn't there.

The service ended and we drifted away, and no one commented on the ring on Mel's finger.

~

A few weeks later we were heading to the reception of a cousin's wedding on my father's side. As we bumbled across London, I finally agreed. We should tell them. My mum was miserable, Uncle Steve was depressed, and my father's side of the family were flat. Even with the joy of the wedding today, which also fell on my father's birthday, there was a shadow where there should have been sunlight.

'Okay,' I agreed. 'Let's tell them.' Starting with my dad at this wedding.

I had a bag of birthday gifts for my dad. DVDs of *633 Squadron*, *The Dam Busters* and some other classics – the films we had watched when I was a kid. It seemed insufficient now, and we hopped off the tube and went into the nearest bottle shop we could find on a street corner in the outer suburbs of London.

'What's the best brandy you have?' I asked, and the chap at the till showed me a bottle from behind the counter. Up high, on the right. It came with its own box. Looked expensive. Was expensive. Damned expensive.

'Are you nervous?' Mel asked.

Damn right I was. I was a lot poorer now as well.

~

The reception was beautiful. My cousin and his wife both looked happy. Nan was there with a cut below one eye from where she had fallen a few days before. She was still adjusting to life without Grandad, something she never quite managed to do, passing a few short years later herself.

Speeches were made and applause given, and a first dance danced. I sat by my dad and said I had some gifts for him. I gave him the DVDs and then the brandy. 'Oh,' he said, looking at it and then looking at it closer. 'Oh,' he said again.

'Meant to be a good one,' I said, and then lost the words to say, *By the way, I'm getting married and moving to Sydney in a few months.*

'Well, we'll have to try it before you go back to London.'

The afternoon moved along, and Mel gave me fierce side-eye. My dad moved towards the bar, and I followed him, tapping him on the shoulder.

'Hey, uhm,' I said.

'You okay?'

'Yes, uhm, this is a good news, bad news kind of thing.'

He stopped and looked at me with a face very similar to the one I have now grown into myself, though his hair is still far less grey than mine.

'Mel and I ... we're getting married.'

Sun shone, straight from his smile. Joy is ever-infectious.

'Oh. That's. That's magic.' He pulled me in for a hug.

'And uhm – I'm going to move to Sydney a few weeks after the wedding.'

The hug hitched. Good news and bad news landing together.

He stepped back and blinked and smiled and told me that he was so happy.

After that, everyone knew, and our two-people-and-a-curry plan became a backyard London wedding: a marquee, my parents meeting for the first time in years, suits, chaos, a paparazzo friend taking our wedding photos, which we wouldn't develop for months until we were in deepest Cambodia. Speeches, cigars, a hangover that lasted days, and then a countdown to leaving the country, leaving my friends and leaving my family.

Two funerals, a wedding, and then another wedding that would've been magic in a curry house, but was a great deal of fun in a London back garden.

My Funeral

Of course I've thought about it. This is what I've come up with so far.

A service in the back garden, since it's nearly always sunny in Sydney. It will be like the wedding reception we had, under another marquee bought the day before and erected at the last minute. The coffin will be wheeled through the garden gate by a funeral home, who will come back an hour or so later and take me away from home for the last time.

I want 'Kiss Me, I'm Shitfaced' by The Dropkick Murphys played. If there is any kind of slideshow, that's the song to put behind it. If anyone is stuck for a reading idea, I wrote a poem years ago called 'O'Toole Tells Tales', a children's rhyming story that I still think is about the best thing I ever put down. I'd like people to hear that, since hardly anyone has ever read it. Hot chocolate could be served to everyone and then, once they are sat blowing steam from their cups, Mel could read my poem. She's got a lovely reading voice. Everyone could lean into each other and sip their drinks for the ten minutes it would take to read. If anyone falls asleep, I really don't mind. I like the idea of the funeral home returning to a back garden of sleeping people, empty mugs of chocolate and a coffin with flowers blowing off the surface in the afternoon sunlight.

I guess I don't really mind if the coffin is there or not. Once my lights are off, I don't have any wishes as to what happens to the building, to my body. Donate me, cremate me, but just kind of celebrate me. Put me in the garden with mushrooms if it is legal. A good end, to me, is more about the hope that people will speak of me with affection. The ridiculous time I was reported missing to the British Embassy in Malaysia, the time my father-in-law saved me from hypothermia by pulling his underwear over my head, the time I was arrested at Bangkok train station. You know, the fun stuff.

There are stories about all of us, and we only really die when people stop telling them. As long as they are still there, even if unspoken, only thought of now and again, then we are still present. Still shaping the future in our way, from the past.

Who knows, maybe euthanasia will be legal by then and funerals will have changed. The soon-to-be-deceased will be there, still living, watching their own funeral and smiling at the stories. They'll be warm and comfortable until the end, when the funeral director steps forwards and presses a red button to release the rush of sedative to slow, slow and slow the heartbeat until, safe, loved and lauded, eyes close. The last thing a person hears will be the cheers and gratitude from their family and friends as the final song starts to play.

Are we mature enough as a society to move towards that yet? Death is still so hidden away, behind the curtain, kept in the dark. Could we be present as it intentionally happens?

I understand that vets encourage people to attend if they are having a pet put down, but some people don't because it is too hard.

The vets must then wrangle the animals who only want their owners there to hold them, kiss them, as they go to sleep. What a perfect way to die, a vet told me once, in the arms of someone who loves us. What more could we ever want?

Would we be able to do the same at living funerals? Hold the hand of a loved one as they are gently euthanised? Be with them for that one last time as the pain ends and the sun sets? It's a dream of mine. I doubt it will ever happen, but I hope.

Please do not play 'My Way' for my final song.

If he can still play it, I want my son on his guitar picking the main theme from *How to Train Your Dragon*. That would do for me.

I love it when Sandy plays that piece. I love to watch him when he sits and strums and then picks out those notes. This perfect collision of Mel and me now fully grown, ridiculous and beautiful.

And I love watching Tilda painting by the window or cooking in the kitchen with a mountainous mess forming around her. A completely different, completely perfect, blend of Mel and me.

And I love hearing Mel beating up the coffee machine in the kitchen as she makes her seventh coffee of the day, while absent-mindedly singing 'Diamonds Are a Girl's Best Friend'.

And I love to hear the dog in the garden barking at a straw-necked ibis that's dared to land on the grass.

I love these small moments, in my home, that make my life.

Look at everything I have – and look how quickly it all rushes by.

They were babies so recently, Sandy and Tilda. The dog was a puppy. Mel was only just completing her world tour of a boyfriend in every country before meeting me and giving up.

Look how very quickly it all rushes by. How quickly we are forty, and then fifty, and then onward with the numbers spiralling upwards.

A man once said to me, 'I am eighty-seven – how the hell did that happen? I don't remember that many years, but it seems that I have lived them. It's all gone so fast.' He smiled, named his children and grandchildren. He smiled as he looked at his wife.

How much fun it has been; how much fun it still is. Even with the stress and the pain and the hope and the loss, look how good life really is.

I remember sitting with Odette before she passed, smoking a menthol cigarette on the bench outside the hospital. A tradie wandered by and winked at her, and she smiled and said, 'Still got it.' I remember watching Chris walk back into the hospital, smiling his champion of a smile and waving to me from the doorway, and selfishly thinking, 'Yeah, he'll beat this.'

Look at Tilda paint. Look at Sandy play the guitar. Look at Mel drinking coffee. Look at the moments that make the memories that fill the minutes and the hours and the days.

A family left champagne for us the other day after a wake, and I gave a bottle to the caterer. I asked him if he was married, and he said he was. 'Go home, pop the bottle and tell your wife you love her.'

There's time to think about my funeral later. For now, there's things to do. Another dad joke to tell, another curry to make, another Christmas with the in-laws with too much cake, another glass of wine and another good book. There's a library's worth of good books still to read – before my finger points anywhere close to the last page and the words *The End*.

Two Letters

1

On a quiet day, I was cleaning my desk when the phone chirped. One of my colleagues took the call and I heard him call my name.

'Lady for you.'

'Did you catch her name?'

He shook his head. 'She just asked for you by name. Sorry.'

I pressed the flashing light and introduced myself, and the woman at the end of the line gave a long sigh.

'You are Richard?'

I said that I was.

She told me her name, which I didn't know, and then said she needed to read me a letter.

'I'm sorry for how you find me, but when you do, please ring Richard Gosling and he will treat you well.'

The letter went on to detail a suicide.

It was a completely unprecedented experience to be the first line of

251

someone's suicide note. I had no way of holding on to the sensation. Was it horror at being thought of so close to someone's death? Was it pride at being considered as someone who would treat them well? Had I failed this person in not seeing it coming? After the phone call, I was shaken and explained out loud to my colleagues what I had just heard, that I was the first line of a woman's suicide note.

'Who was she?' they asked.

~

She was one of my first clients. One of my first on call rotations – a Saturday meeting at her home to arrange her mother's funeral.

The house was freezing, every window open. Despite being a constantly overheated Englishman in Sydney, in this house I was shivering. The woman's mother's body was at one of the local hospitals. We would be picking her up on the following Monday once the paperwork was ready.

On this Saturday she had asked to work through what we needed to do in terms of the funeral, and she ushered me through the house to a round wooden table.

'We sit here,' she said and settled herself, pulling her hands inside the sleeves of her jumper.

'How are you going?' I asked her.

She looked down to the floor. 'I'm not dealing with things very well.'

This was early days for me, when I hadn't learnt about grief fully. I was still tiptoeing around what I should say and how I should say it. I tried, though. The intent was there, if not the vocabulary.

'It's hard,' I said.

She nodded furiously. 'It's so hard. How was I to know? I mean, how was I supposed to know when my mother was too weak to be a mother anymore and that she needed me to be the one in charge? I let her down, didn't I? I should have been a better child.'

I had a sudden feeling of imposter syndrome. Who was I to be sat here in this woman's private grief? Who was I to be presenting myself as the best placed person to care for her mother's funeral?

I struggled with what to say. I mumbled, 'I don't think you let her down. I'm sure you were a very good daughter to her.'

She snapped back quickly, 'How can you say that? You don't even know me.'

I hadn't written a word yet. My file was empty, and her mother was still at the hospital. *Maybe I should give her the names of some other funeral homes*, I thought. *Maybe I'm not meant for this kind of work.*

'I don't know you, you're right. I guess I assume everyone I meet loved the person who has passed. I can't imagine you were ever intentionally unkind.'

She wept then. I sat quietly, not sure what to do. I was so busy questioning myself and my abilities that I almost forgot the simplest thing in the world to do with someone who is crying. Something I learnt from a high-school friend by the name of Ashley at a school disco once, when we came across a sobbing teenage girl who'd obviously not had the slow dance outcome she'd been hoping for. Presented with a crying girl, I had no idea. Ashley, though, sat next to her and put a coat on her shoulders and simply said, 'Just cry, love. You'll feel better.' She wept, felt better, calmed down, and then went back inside with an embarrassed thanks tossed our way.

That day, I simply said what Ashley had said. 'Just cry, you'll feel better.'

For long minutes she cried. Then she slowed her breathing and said, 'I feel like I missed the sign, the sign that it was time for me to give back to her. To care for her. To be her parent.'

I held her hand, and it was icy cold.

'I'm not going to be able to convince you otherwise, if you have your mind set that way, but I'd say you fed her every night, kept her warm – those things are the definition of care. As far as I am concerned they are, anyway.'

She calmed herself slowly, and then told me that her mother was never warm. No matter how many blankets and cardigans she wore.

'It is a little cool in here, I have to admit.'

Eventually we started the file, and she gave me her mother's name.

'That's a Scrabble winner of a name,' I said, and she smiled and told me it was from her mother's homeland. Before we could move on, she suddenly asked me if I believed in hell.

'No. No, I do not.'

'Why?' she demanded.

I was adrift and said simply what made the most sense to me. 'It makes no sense. Neither does heaven, if I am honest. If there is a God, why would he set us up to fail like that? Here are your seventy or eighty years of life, but disappoint me in any way and I'm giving you an infinity of pain and despair. That degree of begrudging, it doesn't sound just or loving to me. It sounds cruel.'

She nodded, and then shook her head. 'No, I believe in hell.'

'Why?'

'I was raised to. My mother: she believed in it as well.'

I thought of my kids and replied, 'If I'd told my kids it existed, then they would believe in it. Kids believe whatever adults tell them.

I think mine might still believe in Santa Claus. I haven't told mine about heaven or hell. I have told them that cheese is a great thing, and that they should always say please and thank you.'

'Thank you. It is a good thing to say.' She smiled weakly. I hoped the topic of hell was finished.

'Do you think the devil says thank you? When a new soul arrives? Thanks them for being evil?'

'We're stuck on this theme, aren't we? No, I don't think the devil does say that. Because I don't believe in the devil. I don't believe in God or the devil.'

There's no manual when we go out on arrangement meetings. Conversations can spiral in any direction, and this day was an on-the-spot lesson in trying to control things.

'So, when we die?'

'I think that when we die the lights go out. What we are ceases to be, and we become memory. Other people's memories. Your memories of your mother are hopefully good. And that's where she is now, in your memories. And one day, people will have memories of you, memories that will hopefully make them smile.'

She sat quietly, and I held my pen, hoping to complete the file.

'My mother was so cold,' she said again. 'She'd cry out at night about how cold she was. She'd say the cold was biting her.'

'Well, I'm English originally. I know about the cold.'

'Mum saw the cold.'

'Saw it?'

'As a little creature. In every room. Every day.'

I was running out of things to say.

'Can I put you in touch with help? Support? I can have someone call you who can talk things through with you.'

She waved away the idea. I brought it up again, but she was adamant that she didn't want such a thing.

We moved back to the funeral, and I asked about clergy, or a celebrant.

'For what purpose?'

'To speak, to lead the service. Will you be saying anything?'

'I am saying it all to you.'

'So do I understand that you don't wish for a service for Mum?'

'Must I have one?'

'No. If you feel you would be better not having one?'

'What would you do if there is no service?'

'I'd arrange cremation. I'd let you know when. What day, what time. If you are sure that some time with Mum – with the coffin – wouldn't give you some form of closure?'

'I was with her when she died.'

'I'm sure that was a comfort to her.'

She shook her head. 'There's no comfort.'

I promised there was. That she could be comforted if she let herself be.

'And if I choose not to be?'

'Then things will get worse, I'd imagine. But I hope you don't go that way. I hope you come out from under this weight you are putting on yourself.'

I offered again to put her in touch with a counsellor, but she shook her head. When I left, she was still sitting at the table in the house where the cold was a creature that could be seen, felt and heard.

~

Eventually we did have a service. A small gathering. I picked up the daughter and brought her to the chapel and then drove her home afterwards. She was calm, smiling, quieter. The service had been small, but it had seemingly done her some good.

At the door to the house, I said goodbye, and she asked me if I would like a cup of tea.

'I can't, I'm afraid. I have to get back.'

She nodded. 'I see it now,' she told me.

'What?'

'The cold. The creature.'

Behind her, the house was bright, curtainless windows and polished floors and nowhere to hide.

'Please, talk to your doctor. Be kind to yourself and look for help.'

'No, it's okay,' she said. 'I am making friends with it.'

She hugged me and closed the door, and I walked back to my car, honestly a little too afraid to look back at the house in case there was something looking back at me from one of the windows.

~

For two years this funeral faded into a dinnertime anecdote or a moderately scary story to exaggerate to my children. Then one morning, she called and asked for me and told me she wanted to pre-pay her own funeral.

'Just a simple cremation. Can I do that?'

Remembering the previous time we had met, I overstepped my bounds completely and said, 'We can, yes, but can you promise me you aren't thinking of doing anything drastic?'

'Oh no,' she said with a laugh. 'No, life is much better now. You were so kind last time that I thought I would call you. I was raised to be organised.'

'I remember,' I said, and a day later I was back at the freezing house, though it was now warm, and back with the woman, who was now smiling and relaxed and calm. She found the process of making arrangements fascinating and asked if she could fill out the file herself. I sat quietly as she wrote all her details down in perfect penmanship, only momentarily becoming quiet when she wrote in her mother's information.

'Dear Mama,' she whispered.

'How have you been? Since the last time we met?'

She put the pen down and told me about working a part-time job. About playing cards with a local group. 'I get out now. I spent too many years indoors.'

'That's excellent,' I replied, genuinely pleased for her.

'And you want to ask me about the little cold, don't you?' She was smiling.

'Well, it is a very memorable moment in my life.'

She nodded. 'Yes. Yes. Not many clients tell you about the cold pacing around their mother.'

I agreed.

'It was all a silly time,' she said. 'I see that now. There was no cold creature.'

We continued. She wrote me a cheque for the pre-paid funeral costs, and I said I would come back with final contracts.

When I returned to her home a couple of weeks later, she took the contracts and signed them. I said my goodbyes and said I didn't want to see her for a long time now, and she promised me I wouldn't.

~

Many months later I received the call. She'd taken her own life at home. She went to the coroners, and from there she came to me a few days later.

I should have been able to call Beyond Blue on her behalf. Log a call and say, 'Look, this lady needs help, please call her,' rather than just asking her to tell me she wasn't planning to do anything drastic.

Really, who would reply, 'Why, yes, I am, I am planning to kill myself.' I'd taken her at her word and drawn up the pre-paid cremation for her, and now here I was driving someone that I guess, deep down, I had known might be suicidal. Someone who had seen the image of a cold creature pacing her home – a creature that her mother had seen before her. Someone who deserved a better deal of the cards in life.

I'd failed her completely, and when I pulled the coffin out of the hearse at the crematorium, I felt fraudulent. This wasn't my fault, but surely I could have done something. Should have done something. To this day, though, I don't know what.

'You okay, Rich?' one of the crematorium guys asked me.

'Yeah, no. Not really.'

'Bad day?' he asked.

'Bad case,' I said and nodded to the coffin. I told him about the suicide note. The fact of my name being on the first line still chilled me.

'Jesus, that's heavy. You okay?'

'Nothing a beer won't wash away, I guess,' I said, trying not to pass on my bad feeling to him.

He shook his head. 'No, I don't think a beer will do this one. Whisky. Have a whisky.'

He rolled her coffin away towards the cremators. I said goodbye and drove back, then bought whisky that afternoon, feeling I'd been given permission to sink my sorrows.

Since then, I haven't become a suicide solution, but I have become far more aware of it. You can't be in someone's suicide note and not become conscious that people are ending their lives every week, every day. I know people have their own reasons for their actions, but I do believe one more sunrise, the right song, sandwich, conversation, movie, anything, could elevate a mood and give someone the voice to say, 'I need help.'

She had been as good as screaming that she needed help, and I'd had no idea what to do. I kept hoping that maybe she was okay, that she genuinely just wanted her cremation pre-planned and tucked away for one day in the dim and distant future.

Did I fail her? I feel that I did. It's the paradox of being a funeral director who would prefer people to stay alive. I'd rather she was still here with her pre-paid cremation years hence. Reading a good book, eating a good meal, shouting at the television when the wrong person wins the best actor Oscar. Being alive.

There are so many tomorrows for all of us, it's a shame to give them away.

~

In a funeral home the size of the one I work at, we would normally see two suicides in a year. Maybe three at most. During 2022, we reached considerably more. Our contemporaries were seeing more as well. The churches I spoke to during that chaotic year of the virus and its after-effects were also seeing more.

I talked to the rabbis I liaise with, the reverends and Catholic priests. I told them all about the spikes in suicides and asked them to raise it with their faithful. I mentioned it to crematoria staff, asked them to check in on anyone who had fallen silent in their social circles. I mentioned it to families as they came in to talk about Mum or Dad. I raised in passing anywhere I could that suicides were on the rise, asking people to reach out to anyone who had gone silent or seemingly drifted into the darkness. Any voice, I am certain, helps. Each time I receive a call from the loved one of someone who has taken their own life, it feels the same: the loss of a life that, with one more sunrise, may have found something better; with one more check-in from someone, maybe they would have stayed.

I see the faces of the families and friends left behind, see the weight on their eyes, the pain on their lips as they say the name of their son, daughter, friend or parent.

He'd been depressed for a long time. She was struggling. They were lost in themselves.

'I hope their ending brought them peace,' I say, knowing it has done the opposite for the people I am sitting with now.

'How are you going?' I ask them, and they sigh. Sometimes they chuckle ironically, sometimes they sob, but the wound they are carrying won't heal over. Every one of them carries the loss way into the future.

I received one call, a woman telling me she'd called earlier about her son and spoken to a young lady. There's a lady in my office, and so I assumed it was her. 'I'm calling about my son, he – he took his own life.'

The colour faded from the day. Shadows stretched. Her pain was clear through the phone.

'I'm sorry to hear that. That's the last thing we want to hear.'

'Thank you.'

'It won't help, I know, but however you are feeling, it's right. If you're crying, it's the right thing to do. If you're eyeing off a bottle of Chardonnay, it's the right thing to do. If you're eating way too much chocolate, then it's what you need. Everything is impossible at the moment, so if you are getting up and making tea then you are doing so well.'

She gave a long sigh and said, 'Thank you.'

Then she told me about her son and about her wishes for his service. She told me about his life and his troubles. We made a time to meet the following day, and she hung up. I checked with my colleague, and she hadn't heard of the case. No one in my office had.

I called back and confessed, 'I think maybe you called us by mistake. We haven't a record of you calling here before.'

'No,' she replied. 'I realised afterwards that I phoned somewhere else. But I'm staying with you. It feels like the right thing to do.'

~

It is exhausting.

Families carry the pain. They try to work it into shapes they can maybe understand and try to hold on to, but then they lose their grip and see it all spill out again.

Just one more blue sky, one more sunrise, and it might get better. It is absolutely okay not to be okay, and it is right – it is absolutely right – to ask for help. People want to help. I encourage families I meet to ask for assistance.

'I guarantee you that everyone around you is looking for a way to help. If you just let them know, they'll cook, clean, cut your garden, walk your dog. Let them help.'

People want to help.

The bereaved used to wear black as a physical sign that *I AM NOT OKAY*, and people would respect that. Now there is this pressure to hold it together, to be stoic and not display grief. It's nonsense. You can't hold in the pressure.

During my youth, mums would warily cook with pressure cookers, and we'd hear urban legends of the pressure not being released and the vessel exploding. My own mother would nervously step into the kitchen as a chicken was being slowly destroyed within the cooker, and she would seek to adjust the pressure as though she were approaching a bomb.

Pressure builds and has to be released. Grief shouldn't be contained; it should be let out into the open and respected.

~

Call someone.

If you're feeling that the road is too long, too steep, or too relentlessly hard, call someone. People want to help. They just don't know what to do until you ask, and asking is often the hardest thing to do. It is not a glib phrase to say, 'It is okay not to be okay.' There are times all of us aren't okay. Friends and family, support lines and churches – they all have hands; let them catch you when you feel you are falling. No one wants to knock on your door and say, 'Hey, I think you are thinking the wrong things,' but I guarantee people will reach out if you call for help.

My friend Meg works on a support line. She's there for the people who reach out, listening to them and speaking with them. She's one of the best people I know. Every one of the voices at the end of those phone lines are superb humans. There's a million Megs out there, waiting to listen to you and help you. Please let them.

If you call someone, then maybe there won't be a phone call to someone like me, made on your behalf.

2

I was told to sneak in. Park around the back, definitely not before a certain time. Don't come in a branded car, if I could manage that. Please don't wear any uniform.

So, wearing jeans and a T-shirt, my file in a satchel, and arriving in an unbranded old people mover that we had, I walked around the back of the building to the gate I had been directed to go to.

A day before, an email had popped up from someone making contact with us through the website. I'm a firm believer that every message should be answered quickly and the phone shouldn't ring for more than two chirps before one of us picks it up. Reaching out to a funeral home is the last thing people want to do. Making an email enquiry could well be the hardest string of words that person has ever had to type.

'I want to talk to someone about pre-arranging my own funeral,' it said.

I copied the email address and wrote back, introducing myself and asking how I could help. They replied asking if I could come out and see them and be discreet. I reassured them I could. They gave me the directions and stipulations about time and parking.

Come through the gate, quickly through the gardens, and then you'll need to buzz from the door, said the email.

I walked through the complex, past neat hedges and walls, surrounded on all sides by windows, behind one of which I guessed was the client I was to see.

At the door, I buzzed, and a female voice answered. I introduced myself, and the door clicked open.

~

Her front door was ajar when I got to the apartment, and she was sitting in the lounge on a large and comfy-looking sofa by the window, with a blanket over her. She didn't get up, and I bent to touch her hand as I said hello. Her skin was cool, and she pulled the hand back under the blanket.

I started my usual preamble about pre-arrangement and pre-payment, but I could see she wasn't listening.

'I want to have everything in place, for when it happens.'

She looked for all the world like she was just having a rest, but I realised she wasn't. She was drawing near the end. Minutes and hours were passing too quickly for her, while for the rest of us they sprawled out ahead through the days of the week.

'We can do that,' I said and took out my file.

'We'll need to start with the Births, Deaths and Marriages information that—'

'You'll need for my death certificate.'

I nodded. 'I'm afraid so, yes.'

I wrote down her answers: parents' information, town of birth, marriage history, and then her children. She smiled as she said each name, asked me if I needed to know grandchildren and, though I didn't, I let her talk me through them one by one.

'You're a yiayia?' I asked and she smiled at me.

'I am.' She let her breath slow for a moment. Then she told me her daughters lived in the same building and would chase me out if they knew I was here. 'They still think I am going to beat this.'

'Well, maybe you will.'

She shook her head slightly. 'I won't. But that's okay. It's okay now. If I can know this is in place, then I will feel better.'

We worked through her funeral plan – the church and coffin and flowers – and then she asked that her family follow on to the crematorium.

'Are you sure? Most services end at the church.'

She shook her head. 'No, I want my daughters to come to the crematorium with me.'

I mentally filed this away as something to discuss with the family when the time came.

We talked for a little longer, her wanting to know how things worked when she died, who would collect her, where she would be held, how long after death the funeral would take place.

Then she talked about her priest and asked me to let him know about these arrangements but to ask him please not to tell the girls. I said I would try. Then she looked at the clock and told me I should go soon.

'My girls will be coming back.'

I put my things away and stood. She stayed seated, and I walked over and held her hand again.

She said, 'Thank you.'

I tried to find something I could say that wasn't hollow. 'Stay safe and warm,' I said, and she smiled.

'Quickly, now. Off you go.'

~

The following day another email arrived from her. There was a Word attachment to it.

'I know this is asking a lot, but please would you read this to my family at the crematorium after the service. It would bring me peace if you would say yes.'

I opened the Word document and read it through: a love letter from a mother to her children and grandchildren and sons-in-law. Beautiful words from her that she wanted me to say on her behalf.

'Of course,' I wrote back. She replied with her thanks.

Her file was keyed into our system and set to one side, where it ticked with its own clock. I called her priest and told him about the meeting, and he listened to me quietly, and then said, 'I will pray for her, and when the time comes, we will honour her,' and then he wished me well.

She faded from my mind, until the phone rang months later to tell us she had passed. Her brother advised us that she had worked up a pre-arrangement with someone there called Richard.

I called.

He said he knew little about the arrangement beyond that his sister had told him she had met with me. He asked that I come to her apartment to meet with the family that day and told me the address.

'I know it,' I said.

~

Typically, when we meet a family, we have maybe a minute to win their trust, to assure them that we can look after their mother, sister, daughter with safe hands and care. Walking back into her apartment, her daughters now present, her brother there, all turning my way, I felt I was on the back foot. They could easily have a distrust of me, a suspicion that came from the fact that something had happened out of their sight, something with their mother.

The corner where she had sat was empty now, and I sat close to there and introduced myself.

'Mum met with you?'

'She did. I'm afraid she had me sneak in while you were all out. She wanted to set things down, and I don't think she wanted to upset any of you.'

'You snuck in?'

'I know. It makes me sound like a cat burglar. She was very precise. She told me to arrive after such-and-such a time, park an unbranded car out of sight, not wear a uniform, come in through a specific gate. She chased me away at the end because she knew you'd all be home soon.'

They stared at me, and I expected to be called a ghoul and thrown out.

Instead, with a deep breath, one of the daughters asked me what was in the funeral arrangement. I talked them through it, step by step, and when I mentioned the priest, they said they would call him soon. I said I had already spoken to him some months before under their mother's instruction.

'She covered everything. Even the priest is in on this?'

'He's been praying for her.'

Then I told them about the crematorium after the church.

'With the priest?'

'No, just yourselves.'

'What? Why?'

'She has given me a letter that she wants me to read you all after the funeral service.'

I felt awful, having words their mother had spoken but not handing them over. The letter was in my pocket in case they insisted on having it now.

'You've read it?'

I said I had.

There was a long exhalation of air in the room.

'And she planned all of this?'

I nodded and felt the letter in my pocket.

'Then this is what we do – it's what she wanted us to do. There's nothing bad in the letter?'

'Nothing at all.'

Eyes watched me, and then they agreed, and they signed the papers I needed.

~

After the service, as friends gathered around the hearse, I explained to the crowd that the family would now be moving on for a private cremation, but that they were all invited to the wake to be held at the crematorium.

'Family will join you after a brief private committal service,' I said.

The daughters looked to their mother's coffin in the hearse and then to me.

'It's okay,' I said, and watched as they went to their cars.

We slowly drove across the city and pulled up precisely on time at the crematorium chapel. We carried her in, and the concierge asked me if there was music.

'No, just me and a letter.'

She watched the family file in and take their seats, and then touched my elbow and wished me luck. Crematorium concierges have given me some of the most needed hugs I have ever had after particularly hard services.

Standing at the lectern, I introduced myself, and again explained that their mother had me sneak into their building and plan her funeral out of their sight.

'Then, the day after we met, she emailed me this letter and asked that I read it when we reached this point. I have copies for you all once I have read it out. I hope this is okay with you all. Please forgive your mother's words coming from a middle-aged man's mouth.'

I unfolded the letter I had read aloud a few times to practise, so as not to stammer or mumble. Now, with her daughters in front of me, I could barely say a word.

The letter was nothing but love. Her love for them. Her joy for them. Her love for her sons-in-law, her grandchildren. Her life. She adored them all and with her words through my voice this was relayed. Love, pure and beautiful, written from the corner of the sofa by a woman in her last days, who wanted to know that, on the day her family said goodbye to her, she would have the chance to speak to them and reassure them.

To tell them, I love you.

I have loved you.

I will love you.

Always.

I reached the end of the letter and felt my hand shaking. I pulled the copies out of my pocket and stepped down to hand them over. Thankfully, they hugged me.

One of the daughters said to me, 'You will never be hungry if you are near my home,' which remains, to this day, one of the greatest things that has ever been said to me.

~

To express love is a wonderful thing. We really should say it more often.

People tell me love stories nearly every day. They arrive and tell me how great their father was, how perfect their mother was. Beautiful wives. Handsome husbands. Perfect children. Longed-for babies. Such wonderful babies. Friends. Good friends. People who danced, painted, sang, flew, built, discovered, dreamt and loved. There is so much love in death. Pain, yes, terrible pain. But surrounding it, above and below it, is nothing but love.

You were, and I loved you so.

You're gone, and I will miss you.
I will remember you.
Thank you.

Epilogue

For all of us reading this, death still waits. He's still sitting there at the roadside, watching our story unfold mile by mile, waiting as a friend, but often seen as anything but. Waiting, arms held out, to catch us when we finally fall.

Not today. Today is another chance to say thank you. To say I love you. To say I'm sorry. To say whatever needs to be said while we still have time to say it.

Today is right here, and so many things are happening. Just as today is tactile and tangible, tomorrow is utterly unimaginable – as death is also unimaginable. Death, unimagined, can stay far off in tomorrow, until tomorrow finally becomes today.

I was at the cinema with Sandy watching one of the *Star Wars* movies, and when we came out there was a Facebook update from my friend Chris. The last he ever wrote. He'd hidden his cancer from the majority of the world, and now he was announcing it. Declaring that he was close to death. Thanking everyone for their friendship. Asking them to think of him well. Chris said it all in a few paragraphs, and, reading it outside the cinema, I felt my throat tighten and a sob rise in my chest.

Sandy, aged thirteen, saw my distress and didn't ask what was wrong. He simply put his arms around me as Randwick hustled and bustled and people complained that these *Star Wars* movies really weren't what they used to be. Quietly, around the world, Chris's friends all read the same message and all sat in reflection, admiration and grief as his flame flickered closer to its ending. Replies were flooding in, messages everyone hoped he would read in time, before there was no time.

Before he died, Chris said it all to everyone who knew him. While there was still time.

There is still time. The horizon is hopefully far away, although closer than it has ever been. We all look to the horizon, and it's a beautiful thing to see. The sun rising and the sun setting, and everything we can squeeze into each day, until that day.

~

To those I've known who have already turned that corner and met death, damn but you were fun to have around. I loved you and I still tell stories about you.

For now, I'm not going to point to the last words; it's not time yet.

Acknowledgements

Thanks to:

Dale Maroney, Dan Goldberg, Charlie Tapper, Kieran Gibb, Peter Galbraith, Lee Cornish, Chanel Sutherland, Andy Say, Kerrie-Anne Jenkins, Andy Plaistowe, The Wilkie Windsor family, The Smith Burns family, Neil and Lainie Randall, Kate Finlayson, Sarah Thornton, Jacqui Swinburne, Michelle Bova, Emma Fyfe, Lara Cassar, Cherie Devereaux, every celebrant and member of the clergy I have worked with, everyone working within the 'death industry', everyone in public health care, every bookstore and street library I've ever hidden in or around, all at Affirm Press, the movies *Casablanca*, *The End of the Affair*, *Sunset Boulevard*, *The Good, the Bad and the Ugly* and *Ghostbusters*, and Trent Reznor, David Lynch and Stephen King (just on the off-chance this book ever lands in any of their hands).

My kids, my wife, my parents, my siblings, my family, my dog … and my mother-in-law.

~

In a eulogy I once heard 'and there were two words she wanted stricken from the language: bored and hate. She was never bored, and she never hated.'

I can think of nothing greater than this – may you never be bored and may you never feel hatred.

Thank you.